Improve Your Life

Through Dowsing

(Your textbook and guide to dowsing knowledge)

Improve Your Life

Through Dowsing

(Your textbook and guide to dowsing knowledge)

David Allen Schultz

One World Press 2000

Printed in the United States of America

ISBN 0-9700613-0-7

One World Press
P.O. Box 2501
Prescott, AZ 86302
800-250-8171

CONTENTS

ACKNOWLEDGMENTS

I don't know about other authors, but for me, I was very nervous about what others would think of what I wrote. Thank goodness for great friends that provided me with a lot of moral support. Now that my book is completed, I feel great.

There are some people that I want to publicly thank. First, I want to thank Cathy Cromell. Her review of my very first draft resulted in increasing my awareness that I needed to write differently for a book compared to business letter writing. I thank Robert and Mary Ann Detzler, Walter Woods, Ed Stillman, and Amy Martinez for reviewing a draft copy of my book. Your comments were very valuable. A special thanks goes to Kathleen Butler for reviewing and commenting on a couple of drafts. There are two people that deserve my deepest appreciation and thanks. Mary Marie Satterlee reviewed two draft copies and provided me with understanding and clarity for some parts of my book. Dr. Jo Johnson reviewed many draft copies of my book and also provided me with the understanding and clarity of things that I have included in addition to much appreciated emotional support. Thank you Jo.

What ever you do,

Dowsing will enable you

to do it *better*.

Improve Your Life Through Dowsing

PREFACE

Have you wondered what you should be doing with
your life, not only from the standpoint of an occupa-
tion, but to fulfill your goals and dreams? We all have
a mission to accomplish while we are in this physical
form we call our body. It doesn't have to be a grandi-
ose mission, like discovering a cure for some disease.
Raising children to become happy, well adjusted
adults or learning unconditional love can be just as
important.

The beginning of my mission started many years
ago when a woman leading a weekly herbal discus-
sion meeting stated that Robert Detzler, a retired
Unity Minister, was coming to Phoenix to give an
energy-dowsing workshop on Spiritual Response
Therapy (SRT). She explained that the purpose of SRT
is to research reasons why people have problems in
their life and then work with High Self to eliminate
this detrimental (negative) energy so the body can
make a beneficial (positive) energy shift and self heal.
The workshop sounded very interesting, however it
was out of my financial means.

At that time, my life was very frustrating. My six-
year relationship with my girlfriend ended in a stormy

and expensive separation. I came home from work one day and she was gone, along with most of our possessions. I was forced to sell our home and made zero profit. I moved into a rental condominium with a bed, card table, one folding chair and a large credit card debt. I was very angry and depressed. My paychecks barely made it to the next payday. There was no disposable income for purchasing furniture, let alone spending money for a workshop.

Each month, I mailed my rent check to the condominium owner. However, a month before the workshop, my rent check came back marked "No Forwarding Address." This seemed very strange to me that the owner would not leave a forwarding address and deny himself rental income. Since there was no way for me to contact the condominium owner, there was this unexpected money still in my bank account. The temptation to spend it for furniture and other things was great. However something inside me told me to apply the rent check toward the workshop. Purchasing furniture and other things would have to wait. Having this extra money was a miracle from the universe. Being able to take the SRT workshop was a sign to me that the universe wanted me to learn dowsing.

At the workshop, Robert gave a dowsing demonstration with his pendulum. He made dowsing look easy and the things he did with his pendulum mesmerized me. Have you ever gone to a place for the first time and have the feeling you were there before? This is the feeling that came over me while watching Robert dowse. It was a knowingness that I had been a dowser before, and yet in this life, it was new to me. He handed the participants pendulums and asked each of us to determine our *Yes* and *No* responses. My pendulum would not move in any direction. Robert dowsed my subconscious mind as to why my pendulum would not move.

He determined the problem to be four past lives in which people killed me for being a dowser. They thought my dowsing was evil. This explained my attraction to dowsing and also why my pendulum did not move. Since my subconscious mind knew I had been killed in past lives due to my dowsing, it was fearful that learning to dowse would result in my death in this life.

Robert had his High Self clear the detrimental energies from those past four lives. All he did was ask his High Self to do this and it did the clearing. It seemed too easy that by him just asking his High Self to do a clearing that it would make any difference. While this clearing was being performed, there was no noticeable feeling going on in my body. Therefore, I did not expect any change to my inability to make my pendulum move. He then asked me to try my pendulum again. Much to my delight, my pendulum began to move. It is difficult to put into words the incredible feeling in seeing your pendulum move for the first time. It seemed magical.

After that workshop, my desire to become a good dowser became an obsession. I spent many hours practicing with my pendulum in doing SRT work for others and myself. This dedication resulted in my receiving quicker and greater *Yes, No, Clearing* and

Research responses. These responses are defined in Chapter Three. It also resulted in my becoming more psychic. Words of incredible insight about people I had never met before came rolling off my tongue. I knew it was my High Self providing me with this information.

It's amazing how an experience or an event can change your life. In looking back, learning how to dowse was a major turning point in my life. This workshop convinced me that dowsing would always be a major part of my life. Through dowsing, my financial situation improved, my attitude was no longer negative, my outlook on life became positive, my intuition increased and my spirituality was greatly heightened.

Most people associate dowsing with determining the best place to drill for water. For me, water dowsing is just a small part of the dowsing services that I provide for people.

I use dowsing every day of my life in many enriching and wonderful ways. My day begins by dowsing the necessary supplements my body needs and in what quantities. When it comes to eating, my food is dowsed for its safety. As various situations come up throughout the day, I dowse for the best way to handle them. One of my responsibilities at work is to determine if people qualify for the City of Glendale, Arizona landscape rebate program. Square footage figures of people's yards are needed. With many lots being pie shaped and irregular, and grass areas being all kinds of shapes, determining the square footage figures by somehow trying to measure them, seemed futile. Dowsing the needed square footage figures has made me more productive.

As you read this book, please keep an open mind to the many possibilities for your dowsing. You are adding a wonderful tool to your life that can provide you with information to help you make better decisions about your life. Good luck.

INTRODUCTION

Dowsing has been a big part of my life for many years. Over the years, I have had a chance to meet, observe and read about some very gifted and successful dowsers, i.e., Walt Woods, Harold McCoy, Robert Detzler, Ed Stillman, Mary Marie Satterlee and Joey Korn. Reading about and talking to dowsers has increased my fascination and appreciation with the field of dowsing.

My early years as a dowser probably reflected the typical beginner in the hope that no one would see me dowsing. Being timid and shy, I wondered what people would think if they saw me dowsing. How foolish I must have appeared to them. The thought of people thinking it was ridiculous was embarrassing to me.

Today, my confidence level is so secure, people's negative comments or thoughts toward my dowsing no longer bother me. Since my life has become so busy, utilizing inactive times throughout the day, i.e., dowsing at airports while waiting for my airplane or in doctor's waiting rooms, enables me to utilize my time more effectively. It is very gratifying to me when people ask about what I'm doing or comment they know of people who are dowsers. It gives me the opportunity to talk to them about dowsing.

As my knowledge of dowsing increased, it became apparent to me that more people need to know about this wonderful gift from the universe. During this time, my teaching skills were being polished through teaching low water-use landscaping classes for the City of Glendale, Arizona and SRT dowsing classes. My confidence level about teaching dowsing classes was increasing, but would the community colleges allow me to teach? With self-assurance and outlines, I contacted community colleges about teaching dowsing classes. Much to my surprise, they were more receptive than anticipated. So far, five community colleges offer my "Beginning Dowsing" and "Dowsing to Improve Your Health" classes. The attendance at these classes has been great. One of the best comments I have received from a student was how much he appreciated my having the courage to teach dowsing. He felt the conservative nature of the community colleges would never allow such a topic to be taught.

The public is showing great *interest* in dowsing. In a talk I gave at the Glendale, Arizona Main Public Library, over 250 people attended while many were turned away at the door because the room was packed. Why are people so fascinated by dowsing? My thought is it opens us to the knowledge of the universe to help us make better decisions about our lives. Plus, we are all looking for *answers* to why we are having *problems* in our lives. If there is *something* that can help us in our decision-making process and provide us with the opportunity to *overcome* these problems, then why not explore it? This something is *dowsing* and it is becoming more popular as people develop a greater understanding of it and how to use it.

Dowsing has exposed me to many interesting situations and fascinating people, which have resulted in increasing my knowledge of life. Throughout this book, I will share some of these interesting dowsing situations about some wonderful people. Hopefully, these experiences will result in your learning more about dowsing and how you might apply your dowsing skills.

My High Self has a way of prodding and pushing when it wants me to do something. The feeling of writing a dowsing book grew strong within me a few years ago. However, I procrastinated in doing anything about it. I have never written a book. But my High Self can be persistent. The more I taught, the more my students commented that a lot of information was presented in a short amount of time. Not all students are good note takers. Many felt they may have missed some valuable information. They encouraged me to think about putting this information in a book. This feedback solidified my confidence with the knowing that I could and should write this dowsing book.

Throughout this book, the word "we" rather than "I" is used to describe my communication with God/Spirit and my High Self. I know that my dowsing success does not come from me alone. It is God/Spirit and my High Self working with my subconscious mind that makes my dowsing instruments move.

When giving talks or teaching dowsing, people frequently ask me the same questions. For example, they ask which is the best pendulum to use and do L-rods need to be a certain length? Some of these questions are based upon things they have read or heard, which results in belief systems about dowsing and its instruments. It is these beliefs, in my opinion, that may become limiting to them and the dowsing process. These questions will be addressed in more detail in Chapter Two.

Learning dowsing correctly is very important. Therefore, my reasons for writing this book are first, to provide a successful step-by-step process to get new people to become dowsers. I have taught hundreds of people how to successfully dowse. From success comes confidence. Secondly, to share my thoughts on what to do if you have problems dowsing. Some people, when expose to dowsing, pick it up quickly and have no problems making their dowsing instruments move. Others may run into problems (blocks) in learning how to dowse. If people become frustrated with their dowsing, they may stop. I want everyone who wants to learn dowsing to become successful at it. Third, to share my dowsing experiences, which hopefully may result in expanding your awareness and interest to the many things that can be dowsed. The more things that can be dowsed, the more fun dowsing becomes.

The main point emphasized in this book is: *Whatever you do, dowsing will enable you to do it better.* Why? Dowsing connects you to the knowledge of the universe to help you make better decisions about your life. It is this better decision-making process that enables you to be in control of your life and take back your power rather than give it away to others.

Dowsing is easy to learn. However, it is important to learn tried and true basic procedures that provide a solid foundation upon which you can build your dowsing experiences. Once you have learned the basics of dowsing, your confidence in dowsing will increase.

It is my premise that we are all born with an innate ability to dowse. It is just a matter of practicing to develop this gift. As your dowsing skill increases, you may come to the same realization that many of us have expressed: *I wish I had learned dowsing a long time ago.*

Most people associate dowsing with locating where to drill for water. Dowsing is much more than this. While water well dowsing is a part of my provided services, over ninety-five percent of my dowsing is energy dowsing.

My definition of energy dowsing is connecting our energy to the energies of people, animals, and things through our dowsing process. From this energy connection comes answers to our questions that help us make better decisions about our relationship with these things. In my opinion, everything on earth is made up of energy and we are all connected by it. Through this energy connection, we are able to work with it to clear or change detrimental energy to help heal people, animals and the planet in general.

An energy dowsing demonstration I teach in my classes is using my L-rods, one type of dowsing instrument, to determine the outer limits of a person's energy field. We all have an energy field, which can vary in size depending on our positive nature and spirituality. Generally it is two to four feet in size around a person. When walking toward a volunteer student, I ask my High Self to cross my L-rods in front of me when I come in contact with the outer limits of his or her energy field. Next, I have him say to himself, either verbally or silently, "This is for demonstration purposes only," and then have him think of a very negative thought. The reason for saying "This is for demonstration purposes only" is to prevent more detrimental energy from being stored within his body. What we say and think is stored in our subconscious mind. Now, when I walk toward this person, his energy field collapses to where my L-rods almost touch him when they cross. This is a very common response for most people. Next, I ask him to think of the most positive, loving thought possible. A considerable distance is needed between us. When walking toward him again, my L-rods show that his energy field has more than doubled from the first demonstration. If you try this demonstration with someone, please keep this point in mind. When walking toward someone to measure their energy field with a positive thought, your L-rods may not cross. If this happens, you may have started your walk all ready in their energy field. Backup and allow a considerable distance between you and your subject. Some people can produce an incredibly large beneficial (positive) energy field.

Hopefully, what you have read so far is getting

you excited about dowsing. There is so much information to share with you. That is why writing this book was fun and my hope is you will enjoy it. As you read, expand your thinking about the many ways to use dowsing. The knowledge of the universe will reveal it to you. Just ask.

Chapter One

WHAT IS DOWSING?

Dowsing, sometimes referred to as water witching or divining, is the ancient art of finding water, minerals, lost objects and much more using dowsing instruments, which will be discussed in Chapter Two. Walt Woods, past President of the American Society of Dowsers, comments in his book *A Letter to Robin* that dowsing activates our God-given natural magnetic, electromagnetic and other unknown energy sources between the dowser and the object or requested information. His definition is technically more accurate then my simple definition of dowsing, tapping into the knowledge of the universe to receive answers to our questions.

Many people ask me how did dowsing get its name? The December 1998 *New Zealand Society of Dowsing & Radionics Publication* provides the following story. King Henry VIII hired many people to help him locate treasure buried by England's pre-Christian Kings. He needed money to finance his military campaigns and romantic adventures. One of the people hired was George Dowsing. Mr. Dowsing used rods that bobbed whenever he walked over precious metals. History does not record his successes, but he must have struck pay dirt often enough for his name to be forever associated with finding things underground using sticks, rods or plumb bobs. Even though George Dowsing is credited for this energy practice of locating things, dowsing has been a part of our history beginning approximately three thousand years B.C. According to an article by Bob Ater, published in the Spring 1999 *Quarterly Digest* from the American Dowser, a pendulum was discovered that belonged to Pharoh Tutankhamen who reigned from 1334 – 1325 B.C. It was made of stone and dangled from the end of an engraved wooden rod. The rod was inscribed with hieroglyphics, which told of a dedication to Pharoh Thutmose IV. The fact that this instrument was dedicated to an ancestor seems to show that it was a very sacred and may have even been used as a spiritual contact between Tut and his ancestor Thutmose IV.

When I talk to people about dowsing, they want to know how it works. In a study described in the Spring 1998 *Quarterly Digest* from the American Dowser, by Ed Stillman, brain wave patterns were analyzed from eight dowsers. The purpose of the study was to determine whether dowser's brainwave characteristics could be measured when they are actively dowsing. Each dowser's brainwave patterns were measured by using a modern, computer-controlled electroencephalograph (EEG), which can produce color pictures of the brainwave patterns while the dowser is actually dowsing. Brainwave frequencies are measured in cycles per second and are expressed in Hertz (Hz).

Delta dominance, 0.5 – 4 Hz, is normally found in deep dreamless sleep. Theta dominance, 4 – 8 Hz, is a subconscious mind-state characterized by lost in thought images and in half awake states just before or after sleep. Alpha dominance, 8 – 12 Hz, is described as an awake state of quiet inner awareness and rest when not responding to stimuli from outside or inside the mind. Beta dominance, 12 – 26 Hz, is the awake brain rhythm when attention is focused on the outside world, in activities such as reading or processing visual information. It appears in problem solving such as doing math or when the dowser is asking questions and receiving answers from dowsing.

The measurements of the dowsers' brain wave responses show that dowsers are in a true and creative altered state of consciousness while dowsing. The dowsers' brain waves while dowsing are equivalent to brain wave responses associated with highly focused attention, an awake state of quiet inner awareness. A subconscious mind-state providing deep meditation, and an unconscious mind state which underlies our intuition, our empathy, and our instinctual action. All of these mind-states have been found active at the same time. This means the dowser is in Beta, Alpha, Theta and Delta brain wave states simultaneously while fully awake and dowsing.

The study indicates that dowsers are capable of shifting to a different and unique mental state with apparent ease. These brain gymnastics keep them thinking about new things and constantly trying new ideas. Once these globally expanded dowsing brain wave patterns are learned by repeated dowsing, they are constantly reinforced as the dowser's skill increases and improves. These dowsing brain wave patterns become a part of the their daily life. This is when dowsing becomes fun and beneficial in helping the dowser make better decisions about life.

Dowsing is an art in addition to being a science. This is why dowsers can get different answers to the same question. When my students use *Chart 1 – Number and Yes/No Chart* in the Appendix section to dowse the energy impact of various colors on them, the responses will vary. With some people, the color dowses out very high, while in others, it dowses out very low. A high number means the color is adding to his or her energy while a lower number indicates the color should not be worn that day. The color is the same. However, since we are unique in our makeup, the color's energy will impact us differently. It does not mean that someone was right and another was wrong. It means that each person's truth for that color can be different.

Dowsing also gets us in touch with our five physical senses of taste, touch, smell, sight, and hearing, plus our sixth sense, intuition. Some dowsers are able to see pictures of different events occurring while dowsing, others may hear things. Some can even taste and smell things happening.

For me, it is the sensing of things, which becomes a "knowing" about what is happening or what has happened. Sometimes, goose bumps appear on my arms, while at other times, a shiver travels throughout my body. These things confirm to me what is my *truth,* which is verified by my dowsing instruments. It is important to understand that beginning dowsers may not experience anything going on with their body. This sensitivity is generally developed over time as it was for me. Some people are more sensitive to energy and experience various sensations going on in their bodies early in their dowsing practice. Remember, we are all different and we respond to energy differently.

There are times when clear pictures appear in my mind to inform me of something that happened to a person in a past life. Many people, including myself, believe that past life incidents or experiences can have a detrimental impact on a person's present life. This is especially true when the incident or experience results in the loss of life. If a wild cat (lion, tiger, etc.) killed a person in a past life, an allergy to cats may develop in this life. If we have taken vows of poverty in a past life, our present life may result in our inability to save money. All past life experiences are stored in our subconscious mind for the conscious mind to access.

The following is an example of past life images my mind sees. A short, petite woman commented to me one day that she had promised to take her son to a rock concert, but she was afraid of crowds. She stated to me that she felt it was due to her being so short. As she was talking, my mind saw a very scared woman being thrown into a lion pit. She agreed to a Spiritual Response Therapy (SRT) session, which confirmed these images. (SRT will be defined in

Chapter Nine.) The research, using a series of charts and my pendulum, took us to a past life during the Roman Empire. She was one of the Christians thrown into the lion pit while the crowd was cheering. This death experience with cheering crowds created a program whereby she associated crowds with loss of life. My High Self worked with her High Self (See Chapter Seven) to remove the past life controlling energy (program) from her subconscious mind. Programs are detrimental energies that cause problems in people's lives. When I saw her a few weeks after her SRT clearing session, she was smiling and looked very happy. She commented that she had a great time at the concert and was no longer afraid of crowds.

Please do not think that you must have these experiences going on with your body in order for your dowsing to be accurate. Just continue to dowse. You will develop your own body experiences, which will be confirmed with your dowsing instruments.

Chapter Two

PENDULUMS AND L-RODS

There are many choices to the different types of dowsing instruments available to dowsers. When teaching dowsing classes in the community colleges, I describe and illustrate how to use the four basic instruments, pendulum, L-rods, Y-rod, and the bobber. This book only covers pendulums and L-rods because they are the two most popular dowsing instruments. It is important to understand that the dowsing practices applied to pendulums and L-rods can also be applied to any dowsing instrument.

People like to watch my hand when dowsing because if my hand moves, they feel that I'm deliberately making the instrument move. It is unfortunate, but many people judge the credibility of the dowsing process based upon whether my arm moves. If it does move, they sometimes say, "You are making the dowsing instrument move." That is partially correct. What is more correct is the energy response from my High Self, through my subconscious mind, changes my muscle tension, which makes my hand move in an involuntary manner. This generally happens during the *Clearing* response (See Chapter Three). Otherwise, my arm does not move for my Yes, No and Research responses.

Don't apologize or be concerned if your arm moves. The important point for you to understand is that you are not consciously making your hand move. Your hand movement is involuntary. There are times when performing energy clearing on people, my arm will shake. To me, this means the person is greatly affected by the energy they are holding in a situation. For example, the emotional anger a woman holds from a difficult experience, such as a physical assault, sets up an intense energy that may result in the woman withdrawing from living her life to its full potential. When she is able to see how much my arm is moving in response to my question, (which represents the intense energy she is holding on this event), it helps her understand how much she is allowing this situation to control her life. As the clearing gets closer to the end, my arm relaxes and remains still while my dowsing instrument continues to move.

Seeing the expression on people's faces is a bit comical, as they wonder how my arm remains still while the dowsing instrument moves. What they don't realize is they can do the same thing if they learned to dowse.

PENDULUM

A pendulum is any object on a chain or string. It can be made from any material as well as being light or heavy. Pendulums can be fancy gemstones on a chain or a simple bolt nut on a piece of string. They can be round, pointed, or any other shape.

Pendulums are my favorite dowsing instrument. They are attractive, easy to use and fit easily into a pocket or a purse. My preference is pointed pendulums with some weight to them, especially when doing chart (i.e., SRT) or map dowsing (See Chapter Nine).

Collecting pendulums has become one of my hobbies. Some of my pendulums are fancy while others are plain. Their composition ranges from wood, metal, crystal, gemstones, and plastic to a combination of materials.

Pendulums have gotten a bad image over the years when hypnotists used them to hypnotize people. This could be one reason why some people are unable to use the pendulum, but can make other dowsing instruments work. They are afraid they will be hypnotized and be made to do foolish things. Some religions believe that using pendulums is the work of the devil.

Everything we do is stored in our subconscious mind. If we have lost our life in a past life that was attributed to our using a pendulum, it can set up a blocking program that results in fear of using the pendulum. Just seeing a pendulum may trigger this program, which may result in people wanting nothing to do with it.

When I teach dowsing classes in the community colleges, I ask my class participants to select a pendulum to practice the dowsing information that I will be presenting. In almost every class, people ask me which pendulum is the best. My response is

"Which pendulum are you drawn to." It makes no difference since one material is no better than another, although you may develop a preference toward using a certain type of pendulum. It is important to remember that a pendulum is a pendulum is a pendulum. For example, don't believe that you must use a crystal pendulum for energy work and a wood pendulum for map dowsing. Since crystals amplify energy, they make good pendulums. Some people believe crystals can attract and store detrimental energy. If this is your belief system, check your crystals from time to time for stored detrimental energy and clear them. There are many belief systems for clearing crystals and here is one example. Hold another pendulum over the crystal one, and determine by asking your High Self/universal consciousness, etc. if the crystal pendulum needs to be cleared of detrimental energy. If you get a *Yes* response, ask that the detrimental energy be removed. (See the *Yes* and *No* Responses and the *Clearing* Response sections in Chapter Three.)

Some dowsers like to use a witness pendulum, which holds a small sample of whatever one is looking for inside it. For example, a gold nugget or flakes could be placed inside the pendulum when dowsing for gold. This may be a good practice initially, but with experience, any pendulum should produce the same dowsing results. When you want to dowse and you do not have a pendulum, use your car keys on a chain or a necklace as your pendulum.

There are dowsers who like to talk to their

pendulum as if it contained the power to answer questions or locate objects. Remember, the pendulum is an inanimate object. The power comes from the God-source/universal conscious, or whatever you define it to be, through your High Self. (See Chapter Four for a definition of High Self.) This is where you should direct your questions.

Some dowsers believe that their legs should never be crossed while dowsing. Maybe they feel this results in blocking the flow of energy resulting in incorrect answers. My High Self indicates that accurate dowsing information will be achieved regardless of whether my legs are crossed or not.

There is also the concern by some dowsers that you should dowse in a quiet place. While being in a quiet place will help the dowsing process, an experienced dowser should be able to dowse in a noisy place and still be accurate. Sometimes you may need to dowse and there is no quiet place available to you at that time. It may take more concentration to be successful.

Some dowsers feel that resting an arm on a table will result in inaccurate answers, due to the table interrupting the energy flow. While it is more natural and generally better to have your arm off a table when dowsing, there are times when I deliberately place my arm on a table to stabilize my arm. For some people, it is important for them to see my dowsing instrument move while my arm is stationary. When my clients see my dowsing instrument move, but not my arm, it adds to my effectiveness and acceptance with them.

For beginning dowsers, I recommend that the chain or string be placed in your dominant hand. As your dowsing skills improve, you should be able to dowse with either hand. Some dowsers are able to dowse with one hand and write their dowsing results with the other. Most pendulums are on a chain or a string about six inches in length. I do not generally recommend holding the chain or string at the very end because it takes more inertia energy (a scientific term related to an object at rest), to get the pendulum moving. However, I have had some students be more successful by holding the chain or string at the very end. I recommend holding the chain or string about three to four inches from the pendulum, draped over the tip of your first finger, or pinched between your thumb and first finger. If you like to drape your pendulum chain or string over the tip of your first finger, make sure you raise your knuckles to prevent the chain or string from hitting them. If pinching the chain or string is your preference, do not pinch the chain or string hard because you want the energy to flow easily. With a relaxed grasp of the pendulum chain or string, you are ready to dowse.

L-RODS

The L-rods are my second favorite dowsing instrument. I use them quite extensively in my energy dowsing work, and when we're locating where to drill for water. Many people have memories of someone with a Y-branch from a tree determining where to drill for a water well site. This process is called water witching or divining. It is important to understand that other dowsing instruments, i.e., L-rods and Y-rod, can be used for locating a well site or doing most any kind of dowsing. (See Chapter Nine for dowsing examples.)

L-rods are basically coat hangers, copper, welding, brass, or steel rods, bent into an L shape and they can be any size. The size does not determine their effectiveness, since one type of material is no better than another. Some of my L-rods are made from welding rods with copper handles, brass rods with copper handles, and coat hangers with soda-straw handles. Just like pendulums, you may have a preference as to the type of L-rods used for whatever dowsing purpose. My preference is for my L-rods to have a metal sleeve over the handle area, which enables the L-rods to turn easily. I feel that having sleeves over the handles helps reduce potential criticism from the public that I am making my L-rods move. When I'm doing dowsing work outdoors, I prefer my L-rods to be a heavier material, i.e., welding rods, to minimize any wind from making them move.

It is possible that a person may be able to use a pendulum, but not L-rods. When this happens, the problem is generally found in past lives. In one of my many examples, I dowsed that a woman was a priest in a past life in which she carried a dowsing staff with her. Her religious group turned against her because they thought the staff came to represent power and control over them. She lost her life at the hands of the group. For her, the L-rods represented a connection to her staff used in this past life, therefore, she was unable to use the L-rods. Once the past life energy was cleared, her L-rods were able to move.

As with any dowsing instrument, proficiency comes with practice. The analogy is similar to playing a musical instrument or sport. The more you practice, the better you become.

Chapter Three

DOWSING RESPONSES

Most dowsers utilize the standard *Yes, No,* and *Ready* responses when using dowsing instruments. To me, *Research,* and *Clearing* are two additional important responses. All of these responses will be discussed in detail in this chapter.

When picking up any dowsing instrument, the first thing you want to know is the above responses. You can accept the dowsing movement provided by your High Self through your subconscious mind for these responses or, if you prefer, program your High Self to have your subconscious mind provide selected movements. Programming your High Self merely means talking to your High Self as to what you want your dowsing responses to be. It makes no difference in what direction your dowsing instruments move for your responses as long as you are consistent throughout your dowsing process.

Most dowsers have some movement in their arm while holding the dowsing instrument. This is their subconscious mind working with their High Self to allow the dowsing instrument to move. Don't be overly concerned if your arm moves some while dowsing. For me, my right arm sometimes shakes during the *Clearing* process. The more my arm moves, which is not deliberate, the greater the energy being held on an issue or problem.

Your subconscious mind contains all that you have observed through your five senses: sight, sound, taste, touch, and smell. These, plus our thoughts and feelings form many of our beliefs that can be limiting, or cause mental, emotional, and physical trauma. Our subconscious mind also controls the complete functioning of our physical body such as our muscle movements.

When you first start dowsing, your subconscious mind can block your High Self and prevent your dowsing instruments from moving. If your subconscious mind feels threatened, it will shut down and not allow your dowsing instruments to move. When this happens, you will need to work with your subconscious mind to remove the blocks and/or programs. (Blocks will be defined in Chapter Seven.) Tell your subconscious mind that it does not need to be fearful of dowsing or answering a very sensitive question like sexual abuse. Once your subconscious mind knows it is safe to dowse, it works with your High Self to respond to your questions. It tells your subconscious mind which direction to allow the dowsing instrument(s) to move. Having an energy dowser/worker remove these blocks and/or programs can also result in your subconscious mind allowing the dowsing instruments to move. A clearing statement and prayer may also be beneficial. You want your High

Self and your subconscious mind to work as a team in responding to your dowsing question. As mentioned in the Preface, when I was exposed to dowsing for the first time, my subconscious mind was not going to allow my pendulum to move. Once Robert Detzler's High Self removed the blocks that my subconscious was holding regarding dowsing, my subconscious mind then allowed my pendulum to move.

READY RESPONSE

Some dowsers prefer their dowsing instruments to be in a *Ready* position before asking questions. An example of a *Ready* response used by many dowsers is their pendulum moving in a diagonal direction, usually to the upper right. However, it can be either to the right or left. You determine your preference. While a *Ready* position works for most dowsing instruments, it is not my preference for using a pendulum. My *Ready* response is when my pendulum is still. With your pendulum in your *Ready* position, you can proceed to ask questions.

The *Ready* response for L-rods starts with holding them about waist high and almost as far apart as your hips. Tip the L-rods down a little to prevent them from naturally moving inward or outward. You can use two L-rods or just one, it is up to you. With the L-rods in the *Ready* position, you can begin asking questions.

NEEDING MORE INFORMATION

A diagonal direction, either to the right or left, can also mean your High Self needs more information before it can give an accurate answer. My dowsing experience has taught me that my High Self understands things on a spiritual plane and most of our physical things. However, some of the slang words or expressions we use in the physical world can have a different meaning. For example, if you want to know what direction is magnetic north, talk to your High Self about what is meant by magnetic north. If you do not do this, your dowsing instrument may point to a street sign with the word north on it, or it may point to a person whose name is North.

Explain to your High Self that magnetic north is like the north, south, east and west directions on a compass, which we use on planet Earth. Then, ask again if your High Self understands your request. When you receive a *Yes* response, ask your High Self to make it a part of its memory. With this *Yes* response, your High Self is telling you that it understands your request. In the future, it will automatically point to magnetic north every time you ask.

If your High Self still does not understand your dowsing request, ask it to find other spirits with the knowledge on the subject matter. These spirits will work with your High Self to provide you with the necessary information.

An example of my High Self needing help came while landscaping my yard. When I asked my High Self if it understood how large desert plants would grow and where to place the plants for an attractive style, I received a *No* response. I then instructed my High Self to find a spirit who was an expert in desert landscaping to assist us with this information. All I did was to wait for a while. Then I asked my High Self if it found such a spirit. I asked this expert landscape spirit if it would work with my High Self and me to develop an attractive landscape. I received a *Yes* response. With over 300 plants in my yard, it looks great and it is becoming a very spiritual place.

If you want to use a diagonal movement as your *Ready* response and also to indicate more information is needed, program your High Self and your subconscious mind to swing your pendulum in one direction for the *Ready* position (upper right) and in another direction (upper left) as *Needing More Information*. Programming your High Self and your subconscious mind merely means talking it out as what each movement represents.

YES AND NO RESPONSES

The first thing you want to know with any dowsing instrument is what movement represents your *Yes* and *No* responses. This is where you have an option. You can accept whatever movement your High Self instructs your subconscious mind to indicate for your *Yes* and *No* responses or you can program (change) them to only accept certain movements.

When using a pendulum, your *Yes* response can be either up and back, side-to-side, clockwise rotation or counter clockwise rotation. It is totally up to you. My *Yes* response preference for pendulums is the up and back motion. This is like nodding your head yes. If you also choose this motion for your *Yes* response and your pendulum is not moving easily, hold the pendulum over a straight vertical line with the word yes written at the top. (See *Chart 1 – Number and Yes/No Chart.*) This may help your High Self understand what you want for your *Yes* response. Some dowsers feel that holding the pendulum over the other hand (palm up) helps to get the pendulum to move.

If you choose to reprogram your dowsing response from the one your High Self and your subconscious mind gave you to a different response, ask it to "Ignore all other past *Yes* dowsing responses." Remember, if you were a dowser in a past life, your High Self may access your *Yes* and *No* responses from your subconscious mind based upon what they were in that life. Ask if you were a dowser in past lives. If you get a *Yes* response, use *Chart 1 – Number and Yes/No Chart* and ask your High Self how many past lives you were a dowser. You might also ask if any of those lives resulted in your loosing your life due to being a dowser.

For some people, the pendulum will move easily and quickly while others may be blocked from dowsing. If your pendulum does not move when you ask your High Self to move it, you may be blocked like my first experience with dowsing. Losing your life due to being a dowser in a past life can result in your subconscious mind blocking your pendulum from moving. There may also be a program(s) blocking you from dowsing. (See Blocks and Interferences in Chapter Seven for more information about this topic.) If you are unable to get your pendulum to move in the direction you want it to move for your *Yes* response, force it to move. You may have to do this a number of times until your High Self understands your request. While your pendulum is swinging, say something like, "From this time forward, I choose for this up and back motion, (or whatever motion you choose), to be my *Yes* response and for it to move without my having to deliberately make it move." If your pendulum still does not move, say something like, "I give my subconscious mind permission to move my pendulum in a certain movement for my *Yes* response. My subconscious mind does not need to be fearful, for I will protect it. Please give me my *Yes* response." I have had many people in my classes say, "Please give me a *Yes* response." If you just ask for a *Yes* response, *any* response will do. I recommend you ask for *your Yes* response.

Once you know your *Yes* response, remember it and always have it be the same response, unless you choose to change it. With practice, your pendulum should move at your request. If all your efforts fail in getting your dowsing instrument to move, you may need to have an experienced energy dowser/worker clear your blocks before your pendulum will move.

Once you determine your *Yes* response, ask your High Self for your *No* response. Again you can accept whatever response is given, or you can program it to be whatever you like. My preference for my *No* response is my pendulum swinging from side to side.

This is like shaking my head no. Using *Chart 1 – Number and Yes / No Chart*, hold your pendulum over the straight horizontal line with the word no written at each end and ask your High Self to move your pendulum from side to side, or as previously mentioned, over the other hand. Again, if your pendulum does not move, deliberately swing it in the preferred direction and say something like, "From this time forward, I choose for this side-to-side motion (or whatever motion you choose) to be my *No* response and for it to move without my having to deliberately make it move." Again, if you choose to reprogram your *No* response, ask it to "Ignore any previous past *No* dowsing responses." Once you know your *No* response, remember it and have it be consistent throughout your dowsing process.

If you plan to dowse for other people, I recommend the up and back motion for your *Yes* response and the side-to side motion for your *No* response. These responses are easier for people to understand your dowsing answers.

As with a pendulum, the first thing to determine with L-rods is your *Yes* and *No* responses. My preference for L-Rods is to cross in front of me for my *Yes* response and to open outward for my *No* response. For some dowsers, it is the opposite motion. It makes no difference. As mentioned above, you may have blocks to using L-rods, which may need to be cleared before you are able to make them move. Again, you may have to deliberately move them in the direction you wish until your High Self and your subconscious mind understands your dowsing request. While you are moving them, mention to your High Self, similar words used in the preceding paragraph, that either inward or outward is to be your *Yes* response and the opposite movement for your *No* response. Have your High Self ignore any previous *Yes/No* responses.

When you first ask for your *Yes* and *No* responses, the movement may be small. These small movements are still your *Yes* and *No* responses. Your High Self is giving you what you requested. If you are not satisfied with these small responses, ask your High Self to *exaggerate* the responses. Now your dowsing instruments should have greater movement to them. Also, the more you practice, the greater the movements will become.

RESEARCH RESPONSE

Most dowsers may not consider the *Research* response a standard response, yet I feel it is important. An example of the importance of the *Research* response has to do with purchasing something such as a VCR. You list the parameters (features) you want in the VCR for the money you are willing to spend. In this case, your High Self may not automatically know this information. Therefore, you instruct your High Self to research all the manufacturers of VCR's based upon the established parameters. A *Research* response is a spinning response either clockwise or counter-clockwise rotation. When your dowsing instrument stops spinning, it will go to your *Ready* position. Your High Self is now ready to answer your question. Next, you start listing the manufacturer's brands until your High Self gives you a *Yes* response as to the best brand that meets your established parameters. When you get to the store, do not just purchase the top box of the determined VCR brand name. Ask your High Self to research all of the VCR's of the determined brand name for the one that is constructed the best. You do not want to purchase a VCR that is a lemon.

Your *Research* motion can be any motion. However, I recommend that it spin either clockwise or counter-clockwise. A spinning motion is fast and very visual. Plus, the length of time your dowsing instrument is spinning represents the amount of time needed for your High Self to complete the research. Remember this motion, because you will be using it many times in the future. When using a pendulum, program your High Self to change the spinning rotation to either a *Yes* or *Ready* response once the research has been completed. With an L-rod, just have your High Self bring it to a halt when completed or move it to your *Ready* position. Once your research is completed, you are ready to ask your High Self various questions.

CLEARING RESPONSE

The next important non-standard movement is the *Clearing* response, which occurs when your High Self clears you, or anyone you are working on, of any detrimental energy. Detrimental energies consist of blocks and interferences. (See Chapter Seven, which includes entities, covered in Chapter Nine.)

This *Clearing* response is also a spinning motion, either clockwise or counter-clockwise, because it is very visual and allows other people to see that the request is being accomplished. In using a pendulum, program your High Self to change the spinning rotation to either a *Yes* or *Ready* response when the detrimental energies have been cleared. When using an L-rod, you can have it just stop or go to the *Ready* response when the clearing is completed. It is a good habit to ask your High Self if the clearing has been completed. When a *Yes* response is received, you know the detrimental energies have been removed.

When it comes to the *Clearing* and *Research* responses, I recommend that you use only one L-rod. One spinning L-rod is easier to control than two spinning rods. It makes no difference if it spins clockwise or counter-clockwise.

A common question that I hear from new dowsing students is, "Why is my dowsing instrument spinning on its own?" If you have been an energy dowser in past lives, your High Self already knows what to do with your dowsing instruments. Ask your High Self if this spinning motion means it is clearing someone. If you get a *No* response, ask a question based upon the first thought that comes into your mind. For example, maybe your High Self is just giving you the visual effect of how your dowsing instruments are to move. Remember to phrase your questions to require a *Yes* or *No* response.

It is essential to remember the following: *do not use your own energy to clear detrimental energies. Always have your High Self do the clearing.* If you use your own energy, you will drain yourself and feel very tired. By having your High Self clear detrimental energies, you keep your energy level high. This also helps prevent you from developing an inflated ego. If you get a big ego about your ability to do this clearing work, you could possibly lose your dowsing effectiveness. For me, dowsing enhances my energy. I have had many all day dowsing sessions with people in which I was not tired when I finished. This is due to using my High Self, rather than my own energy, to clear them.

INFLUENCING YOUR DOWSING ANSWER

Often, people comment to me that they think they are influencing their dowsing answers, because they know the answer to their question before the dowsing instrument moves. While people can influence the dowsing answer, knowing the information before their dowsing instrument moves does not always mean they have influenced the answer. Why? The information comes into the conscious mind from your High Self and is converted to energy that the subconscious mind uses to move the dowsing instrument. Therefore, the conscious mind is going to know the answer before the dowsing instrument moves.

You can ask if you have influenced your dowsing answers. You can also ask, what percent are you influencing your dowsing answers. It should be zero percent. If your dowsing response indicates you are influencing the answer, it is important that you get your conscious mind out of the process. This is especially important when dowsing your own health. The reason is that, you have an emotional investment in the dowsing answer and therefore, you may indeed influence the answer. Dowsing as to whether you have a cancerous condition is an example of how you might influence your answer. You strongly hope that the dowsing answer will be negative. Do not get attached to the potential dowsing answer. It is important to remain neutral or get someone else to dowse the needed information. I tell my High Self that I am an adult and I expect my dowsing answers to always be accurate. Once I know the answer, be it favorable or unfavorable, I now have information to do something about it.

Chapter Four

BEGINNING THE DOWSING PROCESS

Most dowsers follow generally accepted procedures that enhance their skills. However, there are many belief systems used by dowsers that may help, hinder or have no impact on the dowsing process. Through experience and beliefs, they have developed their own procedures regarding their dowsing process. This process varies from reciting a prayer, selecting or talking to their dowsing instrument, communicating with their High Self, making sure legs are not crossed and so on. The bottom line is whatever works well for you is what is important.

Dowsing should be easy and simple; however, it must also be accurate. Be aware of your dowsing process when using any dowsing instrument so that no strange belief system limits or hinders your dowsing success. My goal is more than just teaching people how to dowse. It is important to me that they become competent dowsers. Knowing how to properly dowse increases their trust and confidence in their dowsing responses. The more confidence they have in their dowsing, the less likely they will quit it.

Therefore, when it comes to my dowsing, I have only three belief systems. *First, be in communication with your High Self.* (This is defined later in this chapter.) *Second, be in the clear with your High Self.* (Becoming clear is discussed in Chapter Seven on Blocks and Interferences.) *And third, receive Yes responses to the "Can I, May I and Should I" questions and have permission from your "body"—subconscious; "mind"—conscious; and "Spirit / God / High Self"—super-conscious.* (See Chapter Six on Permission to Dowse.)

Before beginning your dowsing session, it is a good practice to drink some water. Water is a good conductor of energy and it may help improve your dowsing process. Dowsers doing field search for water have learned that becoming even a little dehydrated can cause their dowsing response to disappear until they rehydrate themselves.

When you first start dowsing, a quiet place will help improve your concentration and as a result, it can be beneficial in developing trust in your dowsing answers. As your dowsing skills improve, you should be able to dowse in a noisy place or in most any situation and still be accurate.

INTENT

Intent is a very important aspect of dowsing. What is your intent? Why do you want to become a dowser? For example, a friend of mine caught me dowsing one day. Once he saw my pendulum, he would not look at it. He knew what dowsing was and said, "Dowsing is the work of the devil." I responded by saying,

"Dowsing is not the work of the devil because my intent is to do good, not evil."

To clarify this point, I use the following analogy. With a knife in my hand, I could use it to butter my bread or stab someone. The knife is an inanimate object just like my dowsing instruments. It all comes down to how I plan to use the knife or my dowsing skills.

People are entitled to their beliefs and this was his belief. After I assured him that dowsing would not cause harm to him, he became more comfortable. Later on, we did some personal clearing work on him, which helped him get through a difficult time period in his life. He was so pleased with his change of attitude that he asked me to do some dowsing to improve his business.

If it is your intent to be of service to humanity, then how can dowsing be bad? However, it's also my position this selfless intent/service be fairly compensated. Like other modalities and services, dowsing is an old and honorable profession that provides a valuable service which helps improve people's lives.

PRAYER

Since I am a professional dowser, it is extremely important that my dowsing be very accurate. I feel that prayer helps me become a clear channel to the God-source energy, which helps me focus my energy on what I'm dowsing so that I will be successful. Saying a prayer is my way of showing respect and appreciation for making that connection to the

God-source energy. Also, saying a prayer can help change detrimental energies to beneficial energies. Lastly, but just as important, it is my way of giving thanks for the dowsing gift that God has given me. There are many people that do not recite a prayer before they begin to dowse. That is fine if you feel comfortable about your dowsing accuracy. I have found prayer to be very beneficial in improving my dowsing process.

I like to use the following prayer: "I invoke the light of Spirit within. I am a clear and perfect channel; light and love are my guides." This I recite three times. At the end I add, "My High Self and I are one. We work as a team. Amen." (Author unknown)

Sometimes while reciting this prayer, but generally after, my body goes into an altered state of consciousness. I become very calm and relaxed. Sometimes my body will jerk. This jerking response has occurred later in my dowsing career as my dowsing effectiveness and intuitiveness has increased. You may not experience a jerk to your body or feel any other sensation when you make your connection to the God-source through your High Self. Do not be disappointed. Continue to dowse because you will still be effective.

HIGH SELF

Many people have commented to me that they do not trust their dowsing ability. They say their answers are so erratic, so inconsistent, they feel they cannot trust their dowsing. When I ask them as to whom they communicate with when they dowse, they generally reply, "No one." They just pick up a pendulum or other dowsing instruments and start asking questions. To me, this is where the problem lies.

When it comes to dowsing, it is important to establish your Dowsing System. This is established through your communication link to your "subconscious mind," which represents our body; your "conscious mind," which represents your brain; and your "superconscious mind," which means God/Spirit, The Force, I Am, Universal Consciousness, spirit guides, archangels, or ascended masters.

If you do not communicate with your definition of the superconscious, then your dowsing can be like playing with an ouija board. Any spirit in the vicinity can communicate with you through your dowsing instruments. If these spirits have good intentions for you, then your answers may be good answers. However, you may contact a spirit who wants to play games with you and can now do so through your dowsing instruments.

I prefer to be in communication with my High Self. My High Self is my master teacher within and becomes my communication link to the God-source to form a team to facilitate my dowsing.

It is my recommendation for beginning dowsers that you communicate with and have permission to dowse from your "High Self," along with having permission from your body—"subconscious mind" and your "conscious mind." This makes up my Dowsing System that I make reference to throughout this book. (See Chapter Six on Permission to Dowse.)

How do you communicate with your High Self or whomever you choose? By asking, "I choose to communicate with my High Self, spirit guide, archangel, etc." Using your dowsing instruments (pendulum, L-rod, Y-rod or bobber), ask, "Am I in communication with my requested being?" When you receive a *Yes* response, you have made this connection.

In my dowsing classes, I ask my students to determine for themselves who they should communicate with to enhance their dowsing process. So far, 98 percent of my students have verified that they should be in communication with their High Self. The remaining two percent already felt comfortable dowsing through an archangel or ascended masters.

ASKING DOWSING QUESTIONS

To improve the accuracy of your dowsing, ask clear, concise questions. Incorrect answers are received due to our stating unclear, ambiguous, and confusing questions. Our questions need to be stated so clearly that the only answer (response) received will be either black or white (Yes or No), not gray. Sometimes changing just one word or rephrasing the question is all that is needed for receiving a correct response.

Do not ask ambiguous or vague questions. For example, a vague dowsing question is, "Does my car need gas?" Of course, your car needs gas in order to run. A better question is, "Do I have enough gas in my car to get from a certain place to the driveway of my home?" Your High Self will now determine how much gas is in the tank of your car. It will also determine how many miles it is from your present location to the driveway of your home, as well as your car's miles to the gallon. Now your High Self will do the math and give you a *Yes* or *No* response.

Avoid asking questions that result in an opinion. For example, "Am I strong enough to get through this stressful time?" What is meant by "strong enough?" Do you mean physical strength, mental strength, emotional strength, or what?

Asking a two-part question is not recommended. For example, "Does my car/truck need new brakes and an oil change?" Your High Self may be confused as to how to answer this question. You may need an oil change, but your brakes may still last for a few more miles. When you want to know this type of information, have your High Self first *Research* your car/truck. Then separate your question into two questions. Now you are ready to ask, "Does my car/truck need an oil change at this time?" Then you can ask "How many more miles can your car/truck be safely driven before your brakes need to be replaced?"

Remember to talk it out with your High Self as to why an oil change or replacing brakes is important. What is your criterion in deciding when these things need to be replaced? If your High Self does not understand car/truck maintenance and repairs, have it locate a spirit that is an expert in this area. Now request this spirit work with you and your High Self whenever you ask any questions dealing with maintenance and repairs of your car/truck.

It is also important to mention to High Self when asking questions regarding time as to what time means. This may sound trivial, but it is very important. I like to use this phrase, "in this incarnated body at this point in time on planet Earth" when I'm referring to something about a present situation or myself. Some people like to use the phrase "in zero time." If your time period is not clear, you may get a response based upon a different life.

Dowsing should be simple and easy to do and not create undue frustration. Creating contracts with your High Self regarding having permission to dowse, performing clearing functions, plus other statements, makes the dowsing process simpler. Throughout this book, I will mention contracts that I have created with my High Self. Contracts are merely statements you make to your High Self, which outlines what you want accomplished. Once you have created a contract, you only have to say *key words* to implement the contract. These *key words* are **in bold** to assist you in understanding the usage of contracts.

These contracts are permanent unless you choose to change or amend them at any time. Contracts provide a great shortcut when it comes to dowsing. You can enter into as many contracts as your High Self gives you permission to create. Once you understand how to use contracts, I think you will agree with me that they simplify the dowsing process and make a lot of sense.

Chapter Five

DEVICELESS DOWSING

As you become more experienced in your dowsing, you will realize that you do not need a dowsing instrument because *you* are *it*. Dowsing instruments are visual and help clarify the dowsed information. This is especially true when dowsing in the presence of others. However, there may be times when you need to dowse and you do not have your dowsing instrument, or you want to dowse and you do not want anyone seeing you dowse. What do you do? You can do deviceless dowsing. The purest form of deviceless dowsing is your intuitive sense. In common usage, deviceless dowsing is dowsing without a physical instrument.

There are many ways to accomplish this method of dowsing. One is to just relax your arm at your side. It will move forward and back for a *Yes* response and side to side for a *No* response. Some people rub their thumb and first finger together. The smooth passing of the thumb over the finger is a *Yes* response. For a *No* response, the skin becomes sticky. You can dowse while standing. Generally people will fall forward for a *Yes* response and backward for their *No*. You can interlock the thumb and first finger between the thumb and first finger of the other hand. For your *Yes* response, you will have difficulty pulling your finger and thumb apart from the other finger and thumb. For your *No* response when you pull, you cannot keep you fingers interlocked together. I use quite frequently a one-eye blink for my *Yes* response and multiple eye blinks for my *No*. As you can see, there are many ways you can use your body for dowsing.

Kinesiology, or muscle testing, is referred to as a type of deviceless dowsing used by many chiropractors. The patient extends either arm out to her side, which then acts like a dowsing rod. When responding to a question, the arm is strong to a *Yes* response, which means the arm cannot be easily pushed down. However, with a *No* response the arm becomes weak and can easily be pushed down. The reason why this works is the body responds to *truth* or *non-truth*. Have you ever felt terrible when telling a lie? This is your body telling you that what you said was not true. The problem with muscle testing is the soreness my arm muscles feel after awhile. The same information can be determined from using a dowsing instrument.

Deviceless dowsing can be especially beneficial to healthcare practitioners. My initial exposure to Reiki (a hands on energy healing practice) was fascinating and yet frustrating. My frustration had to do with knowing when to move my hands to a new location on a person's body. For experienced Reiki people, they have an intuitive sense when to move their hands. In thinking about this dilemma, it occurred to me to use my dowsing to determine when to move my hands. Since my hands are holding various points on the patient, utilizing the eye blinks was natural for me. A one eye blink tells me it time to move my hands, while multiple eye blinks indicate I need to continue holding my current position.

Hopefully you are getting some ideas on how you can do deviceless dowsing. Practice different methods until you have decided which method works the best for you. Then practice this method until you have extreme confidence in the accuracy of the information being provided to you.

Chapter Six

PERMISSION TO DOWSE

An important aspect of dowsing is receiving permission to dowse. This is important because dowsing should never be used to cause harm to any person, animal, the environment, or to invade someone's privacy. Getting this permission is another element that makes up my Dowsing System. From whom and how do you get this permission?

We get this permission in a couple of ways. First we ask our High Self three important questions: 1) *Can I dowse for* (whatever you want to dowse)? 2) *May I dowse for* (whatever you want to dowse)? 3) *Should I dowse for* (whatever you want to dowse)? Second, we ask if our subconscious mind (body), conscious mind, (brain) and super-conscious mind (High Self) will give us permission to dowse. Let me expand on each area for more clarity.

What do the "Can I, May I and Should I" questions mean? "Can I" means, "Do I have the ability to successfully dowse in this area?". There are areas of dowsing that require additional training and knowledge to be successful. "May I" means, "Do I have appropriate permission?". You do not want to invade someone's privacy. "Should I" means, "Considering all aspects related to this situation, would it be appropriate, proper and suitable to dowse in this area?". We do not want to cause any harm to any person, animal or the environment.

Let me also answer these questions by giving an example. As a dowser, you have been asked to determine a water well site. The first question you ask yourself is, "Can I dowse a location to drill for a water well?" If you were a knowledgeable water well dowser, you would get a *Yes* response to this question. If you were not knowledgeable in this area, you probably would get a *No* response. Your High Self may be telling you that you need more knowledge before dowsing the best location for drilling a water well. (See the section on Water in Chapter Nine.)

Let's use the same water well dowsing example to answer the "May I" and "Should I" questions. If you, or the owner of the land wants to know whether there is potable (drinkable) water on the site, you will probably get a *Yes* response to the "May I" and "Should I" questions. Water is needed either by you, or the owner of the land for meeting family needs. You are also not causing any harm to the environment.

Now what if someone asks you to dowse for potable water at a certain site. Let's assume you are an experienced water dowser and you enthusiastically look forward to doing this. Much to your surprise, you may get a *No* response when you ask, "Should I dowse a location for a water well." This is when you have to do some detective work. You might ask this person if he owns the land. He may not own the property, but wants to purchase it for less than it is worth if there is potable (drinkable) water beneath it. If the owner does not know of potable water available at the site, then it would be an unfair situation.

You now know these three questions are important. However, reciting the "Can I, May I and Should I" verbiage each time you dowse can be cumbersome for new dowsers. Therefore, I recommend you make a contract with your High Self regarding these questions.

To create a contract with your High Self you ask it for permission to do so. Once you get this permission, mention that you only want to say to your High Self, "Do I have **permission to dowse** for whatever?" When you say these key words, **permission to dowse**, High Self is to automatically research the three questions of "Can I, May I and Should I." When all three questions are *Yes*, then your High Self knows that and instructs your subconscious mind to give you a *Yes* response through your dowsing instrument.

However, when you ask your High Self "Do I have **permission to dowse**" for whatever reason, it is possible that one or more of the "Can I, May I, or Should I" questions will be a *No* response. If any of these questions will be answered *No*, then you want your High Self to give you a *No* response with your dowsing instrument when asking for **permission to dowse**. Again, when this happens, you need to do some detective work. First determine which question (Can I, May I or Should I) came up *No*. Then ask some additional questions as to why it was a *No* response. A possible answer is you need more knowledge in this area before your High Self will allow you to dowse. Another possible reason is your dowsing question is an invasion of someone's privacy.

The same principle applies to getting permission from your subconscious mind, conscious mind and super-conscious mind (High Self). Ask your High Self for permission to expand your present contract to receive approval from your three minds to work together when asking for **permission to dowse**. A *Yes* response means all three minds give approval for you to dowse for whatever. If anyone of the minds has a problem (block) in dowsing a certain topic, it is to give you a *No* response when you ask for **permission to dowse**. However, since your contract is with your High Self, you want it to be the controlling mind in giving you a response.

When a *No* response is received to your request for **permission to dowse**, you do not know if it has to do with the "Can I, May I or Should I," or whether it applies to the subconscious, conscious or super-conscious. A quick way I determine which one is blocking is to have my High Self move my dowsing instrument from a *Yes* movement, to the left meaning a *No* for "Can I, May I or Should I." If it moves to the right, it means a *No* response concerning the subconscious, conscious or super-conscious. Once I know which group is blocking, I ask additional questions until I know the exact one that applies to my *No* response. For example, if your *No* response indicates your subconscious mind is not willing to work with you, then you have important information that can help you go about getting this block removed.

Chapter Seven

BLOCKS AND INTERFERENCES

Each time you dowse check whether you have blocks and interferences, that can have a detrimental impact on the accuracy of dowsing answers. What are blocks and interferences and how do you check for them? Blocks and interferences prevent you from reaching full self-expression. They can come from past lives or from your present life. Just ask your High Self if you have them.

If you have been a dowser in past lives, and if you have lost your life being a dowser, your subconscious will block your dowsing instrument from moving. It does not know that in this life, it is safe to dowse. Your subconscious mind thinks it is protecting you from being killed. If you are blocked, you may need an experienced energy dowser/worker to help clear you from these blocks. Once the past life energies are removed, then your subconscious works with your High Self to move your dowsing instruments.

You could also have current life blockages that are impacting your ability to dowse. If your belief system states that dowsing is the work of the devil, or you don't believe in dowsing because it is not scientific, or you believe that you cannot get a dowsing instrument to move, then you will not become a dowser. Your beliefs will become a self-fulfilling prophecy.

You may be blocked due to entities (discarnates/spirits) in your energy field. Discarnates are spirits who have left the physical body through what we call death, but have not left the earth's vibration. When a person dies, their spirit has ninety hours to leave the earth's plane. After that time, they become trapped and need assistance to go into God's white light. Earth-bound discarnates do not help themselves or others. They need to leave earth's plane to continue their spiritual development. Remaining earth-bound due to fear of going to hell if they enter the white light or wanting to continue to look after a loved one traps them and they will be unable to leave. An energy dowser/worker can work with you to learn the details as to why they are earth-bound. They also have the necessary knowledge and skills to free them by sending them into the white light.

If you have discarnates in your energy field, they can definitely give you incorrect answers. They do this by answering your dowsing questions and manifesting their attributes in you.

If the attached discarnate came from an alcoholic person, the person that they attach to may manifest alcoholic tendencies. Clearing out the discarnates enables him to regain control of his life. Another example of manifested discarnate tendencies can be applied to someone with multiple personalities.

There are many ways discarnates can come into

your energy field. A weak immune system, drug and alcohol abuse, and having a very negative attitude can result in discarnate attachments. They can also become attached by your spending time in hospitals, mortuaries, graveyard sites and bars/taverns.

When performing energy dowsing, Reiki, psychic readings, etc. on someone, you can create a portal opening (energy connection) from that person to you. The portal can come from a past life or the present. Discarnates can travel this portal opening and become attached to you.

Being protected by white light, mirrors, shields, etc. (See Chapter Nine on Entities), keeps discarnates from becoming attached to you. After the discarnates are removed and you have finished your energy work on someone, have your High Self block these existing channels to prevent future ones from attaching to your client/patient or yourself. I have a contract with my High Self to automatically do this. This contract information will also be discussed later in this section.

When clearing these discarnates, it is important for them to be sent to their right and proper place. Since we do not know this place, I have a contract with my High Self to automatically send them into the white light. Then God can determine their right and proper place. Once the discarnates are cleared and guided into the white light, they are permanently gone.

When you first begin to dowse, your High Self may not understand the meaning of blocks and interferences (which includes discarnates) that need to be cleared. When teaching, my students are instructed to ask their High Self if it understands the meaning of blocks and interferences. If not, they are to instruct their High Self to check with my High Self (the instructor) for permission to tap into it for this understanding. If they receive a *Yes* response, they have their High Self ask my High Self to download (transfer) my knowledge of blocks and interferences to them. This generally needs to be done only once. When a *Yes* response is received, ask for this downloading to be completed. Your pendulum should start spinning. If it doesn't automatically start spinning, make it spin. The spinning motion tells you the downloading is in process. When the downloading has been completed, your pendulum will stop or go to your *Ready* position. However, my students are reminded to ask their High Self to check with my High Self periodically to see if my High Self has learned any new information regarding blocks and interferences. If so, have this new information downloaded.

Your conscious mind may still not understand the meaning of blocks and interferences, but your High Self knows. That is what is important. Therefore, whenever blocks and interferences are determined, have your High Self clear out this detrimental energy. When teaching Spiritual Response Therapy (a three day energy dowsing workshop), my students are thoroughly trained to understand blocks and interferences that can have a detrimental impact on life.

Before dowsing for blocks, intererences and discarnates, ask your High Self for permission to enter into a contract for their removal. When a *Yes* response is received, you are ready to develop this contract.

Tell your High Self that you want to use key words to convey a longer request. For example, tell your High Self that you only want to say, "Please clear me, or whomever you are clearing, **as usual**." These key words **as usual** mean, "Please clear me, or whomever you are clearing, of all blocks and interferences all the way to the highest God-head level." According to Robert Detzler, there are many levels of spiritual consciousness that make up the Godhead. Continue by saying, "Please clear me, or whomever you are clearing, through all levels, all layers, all time-frames, all dimensions, all lives, all bodies, all realities, alpha to omega." It also means, "All detrimental energy will be sent into the white light to be dissolved, all discarnates will be sent into the light for God to determine their right and proper place, all dark forces will be removed by Elite Angels, (See Chapter Nine on Entities—Dark Forces) and all channels and openings are blocked to prevent discarnates from entering my, or whomever you are working on, energy field." The reason for sending all detrimental energy into the white light to be dissolved is to prevent detrimental energy from accumulating on our planet.

Your High Self now knows to automatically clear you, or whomever you are clearing, of all blocks and interferences as stated above. Now say, "I choose for this contract to be permanently in place." You can check by saying, "High Self is this contract now in place?" When a *Yes* response is received, you know that this contract is permanently in place. When teaching dowsing classes, my students are asked to verify that the contract is in place. You can say, "High Self, from here on, I only want to say, 'Please clear me, or whomever you are clearing, **as usual**' and you will automatically do as stated above." When a *Yes* response is received, you have verified this contract is in place.

As you become more proficient in using your dowsing instruments, especially your pendulum, you will immediately know when its movement is not right. It will appear to be sluggish when compared to your normal quick and strong movements. When this happens, stop your dowsing. From my experience, discarnates can still disrupt one's dowsing process. Many discarnates no longer want to be earth-bound and interrupting your dowsing process is a way they get your attention. These discarnates do not become attached to you due to your protective shields; they just want to get your attention. As a beginner dowser, please do not let this disturb you. Realize you have the power to free discarnates from being trapped on planet Earth. Just have them cleared **as usual**. This is a wonderful way to help discarnates continue their spiritual development.

There may be a time that you will receive a *No* response when asking your High Self if it can remove blocks and interferences. When this happens, ask your High Self "Is there a block to removing these blocks and interferences?" An example among many possibilities for having a block to blocks and interferences could mean you do not want to be cleared because you need to continue self-punishing regarding some incorrect belief about yourself. It could also mean that a very tragic incident happened to you that is now buried deep in the subconscious mind. The subconscious mind may not give up the energy of the incident easily.

Once you receive a *Yes* response, then have your High Self remove this block. Once the block has been removed, check to see if your High Self can now clear the blocks and interferences **as usual**. If you still receive a *No* response, ask your High Self if there are layers of blocks. There could be many layers blocking your dowsing. These various layers of blocks need to be removed before your High Self will allow the final blocks and interferences to be cleared.

Chapter Eight

BENEFICIAL ENERGIES

When detrimental energies are removed, it creates a vacuum. It is important for beneficial (positive) energies to be placed in this vacuum to prevent any other detrimental energy from filling the space. Ask your High Self if it is automatically installing beneficial energy in place of detrimental energy when it is removed? If not, I recommend that you create another contract with your High Self to automatically do this for you.

In this contract, instruct your High Self to automatically place beneficial energies in this vacuum once the detrimental energies have been removed. There are a number of beneficial energy words that can be applied, i.e., love, joy, success, worthiness, happiness, etc. Since your High Self knows these words, plus many other beneficial energies, trust your High Self to determine which beneficial energies need to be applied. Again, ask your High Self for permission to create this contract. When you receive a *Yes* response, say, "High Self, from now on, whenever you clear me, or whomever you are clearing, of all detrimental energies, I want you to automatically place beneficial energies in its place and have the beneficial energies multiplied infinity by infinity." Maybe saying infinity by infinity is not needed. However, I want to make sure the beneficial energies are maximized to the fullest. Then say, "I choose for this contract to now be in place." With your dowsing instrument, verify this by asking your Higher Self "Is this contract now in place?" When a *Yes* response is received, you know this has been completed.

Chapter Nine

WHAT TO DOWSE?

This chapter explores some of the things I dowse. This is not a complete list, I'm sure you will think of other things. As long as you get permission from your High Self, you are not causing harm to any person, animal, or the environment, and you are not invading someone's privacy, you can dowse for anything.

WATER

Most people associate dowsing with determining where to drill for a water well. This is also called water witching or divining. If you are interested in learning how to become a water well dowser there are some great water dowsing books already written by some very gifted water dowsers worth reading. Also, you will benefit by attending dowsing conferences, chapter meetings (most states have dowsing chapters) and talking to successful water dowsers. Contact The American Society of Dowsers (ASD) listed in the Appendix for more information. (ASD also sells dowsing books and instruments.) In addition to all this knowledge, I would like to share some of my personal experiences regarding water well dowsing.

One of the first things I do before dowsing for water is to establish a list of parameters that constitute a good drilling site. It is a good idea to write out your parameters. This helps assure you that nothing important has been overlooked. The most important parameter is the water must be potable (drinkable). This means it meets all federal and state health requirements and it taste good. Some potable water may not taste that good. If there is no potable water on the site, I ask for any water. Sometimes non-potable water is better than no water.

Some of my other parameters are: 1) Will the site produce uninterrupted water 365 days per year? It is easier to find water in the winter and spring when water is more apt to be flowing. You also want the water to be available in drought years. 2) Is the site to be located on a water vein or a water dome? A water dome is an underground pool of water. Always determine by your dowsing where is the best spot to drill. You do not want to cause any harm to people or the environment by your selected site resulting in people downstream losing their water supply. 3) When tapping into a water vein, ask your High Self what direction is it flowing? You do not want to locate a well site downstream from a septic tank installation. 4) How many gallons of water can be brought to the surface? For a domestic well, five to ten gallons per minute may suffice. However, if the well is to be used for irrigation purposes or a subdivision, you may need fifty gallons or more per minute to meet desired needs.

If only a few gallons per minute can be brought to the surface, it may not be cost effective to drill there. However, if there are other water veins in the area, I ask my High Self if I have permission to move these veins into the main vein selected for drilling. This should increase the amount of recoverable water to the surface. 5) Can a drilling rig (truck) get to the dowsed location? The best site in the world is not much good if you cannot drill at that location. 6) Are there buried rocks in the dowsed location? These rocks might deflect the drilling auger and result in missing the desired spot. 7) How deep must the well be drilled to find the potable water? This helps the owner determine the potential cost of drilling at the dowsed spot. 8) Is there more than one water vein in the same spot? The well driller may need to drill past a shallower vein to reach the desired vein that can produce a satisfactory flow rate in gallons per minute to satisfy the owner's needs.

I ask my High Self if I have permission to enter into a contract based upon my list of water dowsing parameters. Experienced dowsers may have additional parameters they know are important in determining the best water well site. With a *Yes* response, I mention that I only want to recite the phase "Where is the **best site to drill for a water well**?" When I receive a *Yes* response, my High Self is to automatically *Research* the property for potable water based against these parameters and give me a *Yes* or *No* response. In addition, I request this contract to be permanently in place until such time I amend or delete it. I now ask my High Self, "Is this contract in place?" With a *Yes* response, I know this has been done. If I need to add details based upon the uniqueness of the proposed site or the needs of your client, I amend my contract to include this new information. It is important to determine if your contract needs to be amended before your dowsing begins.

When dowsing for water, remember you are the expert and someone is paying you to locate potable water. Sometimes a little showmanship is needed to create this assurance that you have selected the best site for his well.

When dowsing large parcels of land for a well site, you need a good site map of the area. This gives you a good idea before you get to the site where the potential water might be located. This also reduces the amount of walking at the site. For smaller sites where you can see the entire property area, a site map is generally not needed.

When I meet the property owner at the site, I have the owner determine the boundaries of the property in relation to the site map. Using my L-rod, I request my High Self to *Research* whether there are any blocks and interferences that would prevent my determining the best drilling site for potable water. An example of a block is a wife not wanting to live far away from supermarkets, a beauty salon, etc. She may hope her husband will give up on his plan to live there if no water can be found. Therefore, she may create a subconscious block. An example of interference could be a discarnate occupying the site and not wanting people living there. If any blocks are determined, I instruct my High Self to clear them from the site.

Next, I instruct my High Self to *Research* the site for noxious energy zones, which will be discussed later in this chapter. If any noxious energy zones are detected, I ask my High Self to clear them. Once the site is clear from blocks or interferences and noxious energy zones, we are ready to dowse for a potable water well site.

Now, I instruct my High Self to *Research* the entire property below the ground, to determine whether there is potable water based upon the established water well dowsing parameters. When a *Yes* response is received, I know potable water is there. Next, the site is reduced to a more manageable area. This is accomplished by drawing an imaginary line across the middle of the property or the site map. Using my L-rod, I ask my High Self which side of the imaginary line is the **best site to drill for a water well**. Using the side the L-rod indicates, the site is cut in half again with another imaginary line. Again I ask my High Self which side of the imaginary line is the **best site to drill for a water well**. This process is continued until the site is reduced to a small enough area that I can easily walk.

My High Self is instructed to point my L-rod in the direction for me to walk to find the **best site to drill for a water well**. In following my L-rods, they are programmed to cross in front of me when the **best site to drill for a water well** is located. When my L-rods cross, I make a mark in the dirt. I verify the site by approaching it from different angles. Once I have verified the site with my L-rods, I use my Y-rod, another dowsing instrument to double check the accuracy. Since clients may be more familiar with the Y-rod than the L-rods, it is important for them to see my Y-rod pointing down to the same spot determined by my L-rods.

Many dowsers believe that a Y-branch from a tree must be used in order to locate the best place to drill for water. To me, that is a belief system. My Y-rod is made from nylon wires that are connected at one end. With both dowsing instruments validating the drilling spot, I pound a wooden stake into the ground and spray-paint the top a bright color.

Since the owner wants to know how deep the driller will need to drill for water and how many gallons per minute can be brought to the surface, I use the following process. Using my L-rods, we start with multiples of 100 to determine the drilling depth in feet. To determine the gallons per minute that can be brought to the surface, we start with 5 and increase in multiples of 5 until my L-rods give me a *No* response. I recommend that you give a range for depth and gallons per minute rather than stating the exact number. It is a good practice, if possible, to locate a second and third well site location in case one is more desirable to the owner.

If your selected drilled well site produces no potable water, dowse for the reason. Maybe you missed asking something at the very beginning of your dowsing process. Perhaps there was an earth shift from the time the site was dowsed to when the well was drilled resulting in the water vein shifting to a new location. Here is a process I recommend to hopefully resolve this problem.

Ask your High Self to determine if there is a potable water vein close by that can be moved into the drilled hole. If so, then locate and mark the vein with a rock or stick. Ask your High Self if you have permission to move this water vein into the drilled hole. I recommend you discuss with your High Self what you want to accomplish. Through a thought-form process, I mentally visualize pushing the water vein into the drilled hole.

For example, I prefer to stand next to the marked water vein with my arms stretched outward as I walk toward the drilled well hole. I visualize pushing the water vein through the ground into the drilled well hole. Some dowsers pound in a piece of rebar over the potable water vein and hit the side of the bar with a hammer to knock the potable water vein over to the drilled hole site. Dowse as to how many hits are needed on the rebar so you don't fall short or move the water vein past your intended site. Whatever procedure works best for you is what is important. Once I have done this, I verify with my dowsing instrument that the water vein has been relocated to the desired spot.

A friend of mine mentioned to me that his well pump was hissing like it was sucking in air. We dowsed and located a potable water vein close to his well site. I asked for approval from my High Self to move this potable water vein without causing harm to anyone or to the environment. We received a *Yes* response. Using a thought-form process described previously, I mentally visualized pushing this new potable water vein into his existing well site. He told me his water pump is no longer hissing.

ENTITIES AS DISCARNATES/GHOSTS

One area of dowsing that now brings me great joy is the removal of entities (discarnates/ghosts/dark forces) from homes and businesses. The reason why I enjoy doing this is because it helps improve people's lives. People become less irritable and hostile to others.

During my early years of being involved with entities, it was more scary then fun. I guess my High Self knew I would be doing entity removal in the future and protected me without my knowing it. Until I learned about the importance of protection, I encountered many interesting experiences.

Clearing discarnates and dark energies can be dangerous to your health because they can attach themselves to you if you are not protected. As I mentioned in Chapter Seven on Blocks and Interferences, the attached person may manifest the attributes of the discarnates.

In this section, I want to describe my removal process of discarnates and ghosts. I have a distinction between discarnates and ghosts. When entities roam around, they can be referred to as ghosts. If entities attach themselves to someone, I call them discarnates. Since the removal of dark forces takes a different clearing approach, it will be discussed in a separate section.

If you are planning to do entity removal, always check when asked to do a clearing as to whether you are sufficiently protected. How do you obtain this protection? You ask your High Self to do these things. My first form of protection consisted of surrounding myself permanently with God's white light. You can ask your High Self to do it or go through a visualization of pulling white light down and around your body. The thought-form can be visual or a verbal request. It makes no difference since it is all thought-form. If you like doing the visual, raise your arms above your head. Visualize pulling white light down and around you. Make sure the white light is also under your feet to protect you from attachments getting into your energy field from the ground. When you feel like it has been completed, ask your High Self if the white light is completely sealed around you. When you receive a *Yes* response, ask your High Self to permanently keep the white light around you until you choose to change it.

My second form of protection came when a friend one day mentioned that I should place reflective mirrors outside the white light for additional protection. Follow the same procedure as for the white light. The modification I made to the mirrors was to reflect the detrimental energy into the white light to be dissolved. I did not want any detrimental energy reflected back to its source. That would keep the detrimental energy earth-bound. There is already too much detrimental energy on planet Earth.

Some time ago, when I arrived at the home that I was asked to clear, I did not feel right about just entering. I dowsed what I should do. What I received from my High Self was that I needed additional protection above what was all ready around me. I asked what additional protection was needed. When you ask, it is important to listen and pay attention to what pops into your mind. My High Self wanted me to add angels with flaming swords to the north, south, east and west sides of me. I asked my High Self for these angels to be permanently installed when I'm doing my clearing work. When my dowsing verified that I was sufficiently protected, I was ready to go about clearing this home.

At a recent workshop, Robert Detzler commented about the value of having a triple shield placed around us. You talk it out with your High Self how the triple shield is to function. Once you have done this, ask your High Self if it understands your request. The first shield allows discarnates to enter. Once they have entered the shield, they become trapped. My High Self is then instructed to automatically remove them and send them into the white light for God to determine their right and proper place. The first two layers of the shield protect you from discarnates entering your energy field. Again, you can have your High Self apply it or visualize creating this triple shield around you.

When you have finished with these thought-forms, ask your High Self if this protection is now permanently in place. When you receive a *Yes* response, you know you are now protected. However, even with all this protection, always ask if you have enough protection around you for your safety in doing the requested clearing. If more protection is still needed, listen to what your High Self wants you to do.

Most of this section will be devoted to removing entities, which are called spirits/ghosts when they roam around a home or business. I prefer to use the word spirits for them. While these spirits generally do not pose a threat to one's life, they can cause some problems. When they inhabit a building, they generally cause fear to the people occupying it. While my High Self could remove the spirits, I want them to leave on their own free will. To do this, I carry on a conversation with them through my L-rods and convince them to leave. If they refuse to leave on their own, then I have my High Self remove them.

When entities attach themselves to someone, we call them discarnates. I generally do not carry on a conversation with them. There can be many discarnates attached to someone, and I'm not interested in knowing why all of them are there. It would take a lot of time to do this. Therefore, once my High Self has determined their presence, I just have my High Self remove them and send them into the white light.

When I walk into the space being occupied by a spirit that is roaming around in a home or business, I experience a chill to my body. It is like walking into a frozen food locker. This sensitivity was not as prominent early in my dowsing practice. It is something that has occurred to me over time. It is okay if your body does not have this same reaction to sensing discarnates. The important thing is for your dowsing instrument to inform you of their presence.

When we (my High Self and me) first began removing spirits, we chased them all over the place. They would not remain in one spot long enough for me to carry on a conversation with them. Now I instruct my High Self to corral (encapsulate) them and keep them in place for two reasons. First, it is easier for me to verify their presence with my L-rods and my body. My L-rods are programmed to cross in front of me when I come in contact with them. My body will feel a chill, which is another way for me to verify the accuracy of my dowsing response. With my many years of experience and training, and with all the protection that I have around me, I feel that it is safe for me to walk into their presence. Second, it reduces my frustration in locating them. Chasing spirits around is probably more comical than productive.

Once I know the location of the spirit, I talk to it by using my L-rods and asking *Yes* and *No* questions. Talking to a spirit through my dowsing instruments to know why it has remained earthbound still fascinates me. My customers also want to know why there is a spirit(s) in their home or business. The reasons for having spirits will vary. Maybe the location of the home was built over a grave site, or perhaps there was a past involvement of the spirit in the family's life.

The first question that I ask is, "Do you know you're dead?" Sometimes the spirit does not believe that it is dead, especially if it has been killed quickly. When a *No* response is received, my next move is to assure it that it is dead. I do this by walking through it. When this is done, I ask if it now believes it is dead. Knowing the sex of the spirit is sometimes important, especially if it might be a family member.

I always have my clients present to observe this process. Sometimes I ask my client if they have any questions they want me to ask the spirit. Before I ask the spirit to go into the white light, I listen for any additional questions that may come into my mind. I mention to the spirit that for its own spiritual development, it needs to go into the white light to be sent to its right and proper place.

It is important to emphasize to the spirit that it is of no help to humans as it sometimes may think. If a spirit's loved one is still alive, I have her tell the spirit how much she loved him, but now it is time for him to go into the white light. She reassures him that he will be missed, but because he is dead, she will learn to get along without him.

If the person has lived a bad life, its spirit is usually afraid that if it goes into the white light, it will go to hell. I assure it this will not happen. I ask the spirit to call a friend or loved one into the white light to verify that what I have said is true. Once it has been reassured that it is not going to hell, it agrees to go into the white light. I bid them goodbye and wish them a successful new life.

In all my years of doing entity removal, I have had only one occasion where a spirit jumped into my body while I was trying to get it cleared from a home. It startled me as I felt its presence in the form of a cool wave of energy over my body. I got very stern with it and told it to leave me and go into the white light, which it did.

In my early experiences of working with my High Self to have spirits removed, they would pass through my body when leaving. This produced a cool chill when they departed. My friends told me that it was not a good thing for this to be happening to me. The spirits may leave behind some detrimental energy in my body. Therefore, I instructed my High Self to set up a protective shield around me to prevent them from going through me when they depart. Then I instructed my High Self to give me a one-revolution turn of my L-rod when they leave. When my L-rod makes this revolution, my High Self is verifying the spirits have gone into the white light. I like to walk into the space they were occupying to confirm with my body their departure. When I do not experience a chill to my body, I know the spirits are gone. With all the protection that I have around me, I feel that it is safe for me to walk into their presence.

From my experience, it is extremely important to check how many spirits usually occupy the home or business, and how many of them are currently there. Not all the spirits may be present the day you do the clearing work, which would leave the task unfinished. I learned this information the hard way.

A businessman phoned me to describe how his manufacturing plant was being plagued by strange events. Their computers would not work properly and their glass cutting machines would malfunction. When their technicians checked out the computers and machines, they could find nothing wrong.

In dowsing the building, we found five spirits. They

were outlaws who were killed some years ago. I asked the spirits if I could speak to the leader of the group. The leader mentioned that they enjoyed playing games with the computers and the machines by making them not work properly. When I asked why they did not go into the white light, he stated they were afraid of going to hell. Once they were assured this would not happen, they left.

My L-rods indicated that all the spirits were gone. A few days later, the businessman called me and said things were worse than before. He was involved in an automobile accident and one of his workers was hurt on the job. My first reaction was, "How could this be?" The building was cleared of spirits. I told him I would check it out and get back in touch with him.

My dowsing indicated that more spirits were in the building. They were mad because their friends were gone and the building had been filled with beneficial energy. These spirits had left the building before my arrival. Thank goodness we were able to get the remaining spirits removed, but it taught me a very valuable lesson. It is important to ask how many spirits usually occupy a building and how many are currently there. Knowing this information, you have some options. First, have your High Self locate and corral the spirits. Once this is done, you can have your High Self send them into the white light, or secondly, have them brought to a selected area of the building in order to communicate with them. Whenever you are finished clearing a home or business, always have your High Self place a triple shield around the building and set up a committee to work with this shield. When the spirits enter the outer shield, they will be trapped and the committee will then automatically send them into the white light.

I encountered another unusual situation when a couple called for my dowsing service. They said that objects in their home would either disappear or be moved. I found it strange that we did not find any spirits in the home. While standing in the front yard talking, the couple commented on the problems they had trying to get water to stay in their water pond. They first built a pond, but it would not hold water. Then they put a water feature inside the pond and it would not hold water. We were all baffled about this unusual situation.

Their front yard was on a hill overlooking a beautiful valley. All of sudden, a thought popped into my head: We are standing on ground sacred to Native Americans. My L-rods indicated that this was true. My High Self said, "Communicate with the Chief." So, I asked the Chief, "Could the residents of this property and his tribe co-exist on the same site?" I received a *No* response. Then I asked, "Is there anything the residents could do to show respect for his people and the sacred site?" The Chief said, "Yes." He then stated, "If the residents dedicate the pond area as a shrine to his tribe, we will co-exist with the homeowners without causing them any more problems." To dedicate this pond as a shrine, the homeowners were to purchase something that was made by Hopi people and place it in the pond. Once they did this, it took care of their problem.

Another interesting situation had to do with a spirit in a woman's car. She mentioned to me that many times while driving her car, it would just quit running. When these situations happened, she restarted her car and it appeared to be okay. At other times, she felt as if someone was taking over her car, as it would speed up on its own. She also mentioned that there were times when she thought she was going to be involved in an accident. However, somehow she avoided the potentially dangerous situation without her knowing what had happened.

My High Self checked her car and located a spirit in it. Since it was a very hot day, standing next to her car with my L-rods and carrying on a conversation with the spirit was not something I wanted to do.

She had a small, blue throw rug next to her front door. I instructed my High Self to bring the spirit into her home and place it on the rug by her front door. As soon as I made this request, chills went through my body as the spirit let me know that it was not happy about being removed from the car. Normally a spirit's energy field is very small. However, this spirit's energy field extended ten feet away. To get out of its energy field, I selected a chair about fifteen feet away from the blue rug.

I felt sorry for this woman. Knowing that this was an unusual situation we were experiencing with this spirit, it wasn't my intention to frighten her. The concern expressed on her face was evident as she held her hands in front of herself as if to push the spirit away. She didn't want the spirit in her home even though she gave me permission to bring it in. Through asking questions, I discovered the spirit was a male and was also the previous owner of the car. He really enjoyed riding in this car and therefore, did not want to go into the white light.

After a brief conversation with the spirit, I asked it to go into the white light. He said "No." This denial to go into the light after talking to it was a first for me. I could have just asked my High Self to automatically remove it. However, I like to know more information about these situations and, if possible, have it leave on its own free will.

I mentioned to the spirit that it was ridiculous to ride around in a car when in spirit form it could travel anywhere at any time. If he went into the white light, he could make arrangements for his next incarnation. He replied that he did not want to wait that long to be able to drive. He did not want to go through being a child and a teenager before he could drive again. I then suggested he ask God if he could be a walk-in (one spirit replacing another) for someone who wanted to leave his or her body. This way he could be driving much earlier. He liked that idea and immediately left the woman's home. A one revolution on my L-rod was given to me to verify the spirit was gone. I walked to the blue rug without any chills to my body. The woman was very relieved, and so was I.

This incident made me realize how important it is to listen to my High Self and be creative in the discussions with spirits. The important thing is to not panic. Having complete trust in your dowsing skills is important and knowing that you can depend on your High Self for guidance in this area.

ENTITIES AS DARK FORCES

Dark forces are detrimental energies that come from another dimension and remain on the Earth and do not reincarnate. They can have a very detrimental impact on a person's life whether they attach themselves to someone or roam freely in a home, business or selected area. They can make people do detrimental things by influencing their mind. Their impact can result in people killing others while at other times doing illegal activities. Clearing out these dark forces results in a positive change in people's health and the environment.

We mentioned in Chapter Seven (Blocks and Interferences) that dark forces need to be removed because of the potential harm they can cause. However, before getting involved in clearing them, you need to know what you are doing. It is best to have an experienced energy dowser/worker do this removal. Unless you are experienced in this area, I strongly recommend you do not try to remove dark forces on your own. If you still want to do this, make sure you are protected as mentioned in the previous section and have some training by professionals.

When I first got involved in clearing people of dark forces, I did not know what I was doing. I recall an experience of clearing a woman with dark forces without being protected. When I asked my High Self to remove them, I instantly felt intense pain in my chest like an elephant was stepping on me. The pain became so intense that it scared me and I stopped the clearing process. When I stopped, the pain went away. The woman knew I was in trouble and said if I wanted to quit the clearing process, it was okay with her. I asked my High Self if I should continue and received a *Yes* response. As the clearing continued, I told myself I would put up with the pain. It only lasted a little while longer even though it was intense. When the clearing was finished, my pain was gone. The woman looked at me and said in a very appreciative voice, "You have no idea what you have done for me." She was right; I did not know what I had done other than clear her of dark forces.

On two other occasions when we were clearing people of dark forces, there was a blast of hot air that went through me. That also scared me. I knew I was doing things that I lacked the knowledge and training to understand. However, I kept on clearing people. I think my High Self took over and protected me. I also think my High Self wanted me to understand what I was getting involved with since I would be teaching dowsing classes and writing this book. Therefore, I needed to experience these scary situations. Throughout the years, I have learned a great deal about dark forces and I know there is more for me to learn. Since I have had the thought-form protection shields placed around me, I have never had another scary experience.

When you want to have dark forces removed, you need to surprise them or else they will not be there when you arrive to do the clearing. They can read your thoughts when you are in their presence. When I'm driving to a location where they are located, I ask for Legions of Elite Angels to surround the property or person and encapsulate the dark forces so that they cannot escape. Then when I get there, I work with the Elite Angels to get them removed.

I know there are dowsers that call upon angels or spirits by other names for removing these dark forces. Some of the names used are Warrior Angels of The Light, White Brotherhood, Indian Runners, and so on. My dowsing indicates that referring to them as Elite Angels is appropriate for me. I have found that even though my High Self can generally remove dark forces, it prefers to have the Elite Angels do this since they have been given the responsibility to do this type of work. Once you have dowsed to determine the presence of dark forces, you can work with the Elite Angels to get them removed. I prefer to set up a contract with my High Self and the Elite Angels for removing them. As mentioned earlier, we used the phrase, please clear **as usual**. In this contract, my High Self clears what it needs to clear and the Elite Angels remove the dark forces.

A phrase that I use in my contract with High Self and the Elite Angels is when I say **as usual**, I mean the following: "I request the Legions of Elite Angels remove all dark forces from (name of client) through all levels, all layers, all time frames, all dimensions, all lives, all bodies, all realities, alpha to omega, and take them from this earth plane to another universe in another dimension." In this other universe, in another dimension, the Elite Angels can then work with the dark forces and send them to their appropriate place.

NOXIOUS ENERGIES

It occurred to me some time ago that if I can feel detrimental (noxious) energies, then other people are also probably feeling them. I contacted a realtor friend and asked him to find a home that should sell, but for some reason is not selling. He called me about a month later and said he found such a home. The home was completely remodeled, located in a good neighborhood and priced right. It had been on the market for over a year. The realtor greeted me at the front door and started describing the features of the home. While we were talking, I was getting sick to my stomach. I had to move away from that location. Using my L-rods, we found many noxious energy zones throughout the home, including the area around the front door, which we cleared.

Examples of noxious energies zones are subterranean water, iron ore, uranium, radon gas veins, earthquake faults, Lay and Hartman lines, electrical energy fields and more. Locating these noxious energies is a dowsing process called "Geomancing."

For me, determining the type of noxious energy is generally not always important or necessary. I ask my High Self if I need to know what is the noxious energy before it is cleared or changed. As long as you have permission for its removal or change, that is sufficient. Some dowsers claim that noxious energies should be converted to beneficial energies through prayer. I always check as to what High Self wants me to do. In most instances, it has instructed me to have them removed and the area sealed (by thought-form). Sealing is applying a thought-form energy shield over the previously affected noxious area. However, crossing Ley and Hartman lines are always changed to beneficial energy through prayer.

While in the front yard, a neighbor lady came up to me and expressed her curiosity as to what I was doing. I explained to her that we were clearing the home of detrimental energies. She said that the previous owner died by the front door. This clarified why my stomach was becoming nauseous. Once the noxious energies were cleared, the home sold within a week. This detrimental energy clearing process has helped many homes and business sell within weeks.

Clearing out detrimental energies from homes is also important for improved health. If people spend a considerable amount of time (i.e., sleeping) in a noxious energy zone, their immune system can be weakened and they might develop a health issue. Through my years of dowsing, I have experienced many examples to support this.

A retired man met me at the front door of his home in his wheelchair. He mentioned that when he moved into the home two years ago, he was in good health and could walk anywhere. In those two years, his health became worse. We found a noxious energy zone covering the lower half of his bed. His legs were in that zone while he slept.

Another man met me at his front door and said his home was killing him. On a scale of 1 to 10 with 10 being the best, his home dowsed out a minus 10. Approximately fifty percent of his property contained noxious energy zones and he slept in one of them.

There was also a detrimental vortex energy in his dining area. A vortex energy is a detrimental energy spiral that comes out of the earth. I do not know what causes it. When I walk into the detrimental vortex, I sense a heavy nauseous feeling in my body. My L-rods are used to confirm this feeling. Clearing his home was one of the more difficult ones to complete.

A couple retired into a new home in Fountain Hills, AZ. Within four years, they both died. When I walked into the home, I was greeted by a detrimental vortex energy. There were three additional noxious energy zones in the home. One zone covered the top half of the bed in the master bedroom. These detrimental energies were probably very instrumental in the death of the homeowners.

When I walk into a home or business, I first ask my High Self for permission to dowse for noxious energies. Then I hold one L-rod and ask my High Self to *Research* the place for blocks and interferences, noxious energy zones, vortex zones, entities, crossing Lay or Hartman lines and anything else that I need to know. While my L-rod is spinning, the *Research* is being performed. When the *Research* is completed, I ask one-by-one, which detrimental energy exists. I also use my L-rod to count how many of each detrimental energy resides in the home or business.

Let's say we find three noxious energy zones. I ask my High Self in which direction do I walk to locate the first one. When I come in contact with it, my L-rods cross. I ask my High Self if it is best to change it to beneficial energy or remove it without causing any harm to any person or the environment. In most cases, my High Self instructs me to remove it. I do this by pushing the noxious energy to a wall. Extending my arms outward, I collapse it by bringing my hands together. Then I have my High Self seal the area by moving my hands over the area. Again, it is a thought-form procedure. I re-dowse the area to make sure it is clear.

Once my High Self clears out the detrimental energy, I have beneficial energy put in its place. I request my High Self to have the beneficial energy installed to the highest level acceptable to the people living or working there. I let my High Self determine these beneficial energies. Many people have commented to me on the wonderful difference they feel about their home once the detrimental energy is removed.

SPIRITUAL RESPONSE THERAPY

Spiritual Response Therapy (SRT) is an accurate method of researching our sub-conscious mind and soul records for programs (detrimental energies) that are causing people to have problems in their life. The problems could be created from our present life or from past lives. They can be physical, mental or emotional which can block full self-expression. My definition of full self-expression is a person's life becoming happy, healthy and satisfying because our life is working for us. It is also being in the right place at the right time, and people coming into your life at the needed time to help you resolve problems or complete required tasks. Once the detrimental energies are removed, beneficial energy is substituted. This process enables the body to make an energy shift and heal itself.

It is my belief that we are born to enjoy life as we learn our lessons for incarnating. If our life contains programs (problems), we need to determine what is causing these programs and have them removed. Through using a pendulum and a series of thirty-one charts , our High Self is able to research subconscious and soul programs to have the detrimental energies removed.

Here is one example of what is considered a program. As a child, let's assume you see your parents giving (what you perceive to be) more love and attention to your brother or sister than you receive. Do you approach your parents and say, "Do you love my brother or sister more than me?"

Because as a child you did not validate what you perceived to be the truth, you took in this false data and created a program by thinking; "There is something wrong with me." You then put on your dark colored glasses, which represent your *perceived reality* and go through life thinking something is wrong with you. This false data becomes your block to full self-expression. Through *SRT*, you are able to remove this false data and reprogram your mind computer with beneficial words that now make up your *true reality*.

Spiritual Response Therapy is the most powerful healing modality that I have experienced. Here are some additional and interesting examples.

In a session with a woman in her seventies, she commented that she did not sleep very well at night.

The research took us to her childhood where her father molested her. She did not allow herself to sleep soundly because she was fearful that her dad would enter her bedroom. Even though she was in her seventies, the incident of being molested set up a very intense energy program, which resulted in a pattern the subconscious continued to play. Once this program was cleared, it no longer controlled her. When she saw me the following day she said, "I haven't slept that well in years."

An elderly man commented in a session that he was very depressed and had been that way for many years. The main programs controlling his life were hatred of self, not only in this life, but also in past lives. Being a doctor, he was very skeptical that asking his High Self to remove these programs could be effective. He called about a week after his session and said, "I'm no longer depressed." He couldn't get depressed even when he tried.

In another similar example, a woman was suffering from severe depression. About a week after her session she called me to say that she felt better now than she had felt in years. She said more was accomplished in one SRT session than all the hundreds of dollars spent on medications and all the thousands of dollars spent on therapy.

I had a session with a woman who could not eat dairy products. Whenever, she would eat anything with dairy in it, she had an allergic reaction. The research took us to a past life in which she lived on a dairy farm. Due to some financial misfortunate, she lost the farm. She vowed to never have anything to do with dairy livestock again. This vow set up a program that made her allergic to dairy products. Once the energy on this past life program was cleared, she was able to eat dairy products again. Having ice cream is now a real treat for her.

Before getting involved in Spiritual Response Therapy, my life was living from paycheck to paycheck. It was very difficult to save money or have money for doing fun things. In researching the reasons for my financial frustration, my charts took me to many past lives in which I lived as a priest, monk, and other religious lives in which I took vows of poverty. Once my High Self cleared these past life programs, my financial situation changed for the better. The stress of living from paycheck to paycheck is now gone thanks to SRT.

Seeing the power of Spiritual Response Therapy and how it improves people's lives has resulted in my becoming a counselor and teacher. To me, learning and using SRT is one of the best ways to bless and help people.

SPIRITUAL/THOUGHT-FORM HEALING

One of my newest modalities being developed is spiritual or thought-form healing. Harold McCoy of the Ozark Research Institute is credited with sparking my interest in this area. This process is a combination of dowsing, Reiki and thought-form to bring about spiritual healing. While using my left hand to scan a person's body, my right hand holds an L-rod or pendulum. What is comforting to people is my left hand never touches their body. It is held a few inches from it. Some people do not want to be touched. I have a contract with my High Self to spin my L-rod or pendulum when we find a health problem. A health problem could be a broken bone, torn muscle, or any block to energy flows. When my dowsing instrument starts to spin, I focus on that part of the body my High Self indicates needs healing. It is my High Self working with my client's High Self and their subconscious that perform the spiritual or thought-form healing.

Thought-form/spiritual-healing works because energy follows intent. If Jesus could heal people, then why can't we? In John 14, Jesus says, "Very truly, I tell you, the one who believes in me will also do the works that I do and, in fact, will do greater works than these... I will do whatever you ask in my name..."

My process of thought-form healing is to visualize people's organs being healed. The clearer this image is, the better the potential for healing. Sometimes I see dark decayed/dead cells in an organ. When I see this, I visualize my High Self spraying a healing solvent inside the organ. The purpose of the healing solvent is to create new cell growth. With blocked arteries, I visualize a router auguring out the plaque and a vacuum cleaner following behind sucking up the plaque. With torn muscles, I see them being glued together. When a person has pain in their back, I visualize new collagen being placed on the vertebrae, just like a bricklayer placing cement on bricks, and pinched nerves are unblocked. I then see my fingertips (although my fingers never touch the person), adjusting the vertebrae to their correct position.

People have commented to me everything from no apparent health improvement to how their pain was dramatically diminished. Many mention they could feel heat coming into their body from my hand. Maybe it's mind over matter. To me it doesn't matter as long as the person feels better.

Have you ever had what I call a phantom pain? You do not recall bumping or hitting anything, yet you have some pain in your body. I have had situations where all of a sudden my shoulder hurts. When I research the reasons for the pain with my charts, it indicates a past life at the exact age of my current life. I now know that a past life program can be triggered upon reaching a certain age or experiencing a certain event. Then I listen for what my High Self tells or shows me. A common example is that I see a past life where there is a spear in my shoulder. I visualize pulling out the spear. When the spear is removed, my pain instantly goes away.

There are an increasing number of people doing thought-form/spiritual healing work and many are blessed with the gift of healing. You may feel foolish doing something like this at first, however, please don't quit. I have gone through all those foolish feelings in doing this work. The bottom line is to develop skills that may work for you. You also need to use common sense in this area so as to not jeopardize someone's health. It is important, in some cases, that you recommend to your clients that they have their doctor monitor them after a session. As people heal, you want their doctor involved in their healing process.

HEALTHCARE PRACTITIONERS

Since becoming an adult, having a family doctor has never been a high priority with me. It has been my fortune to not need a doctor very often. The times when a doctor was needed, my dowsing selected one from the yellow pages of the telephone book. The selection process is similar to the described procedures stated throughout the book. You determine the important parameters you are looking for in a doctor, such as medical knowledge, openness to alternative health practices, pleasant personality, ease of travel time from my home or work, costs, etc.

I recently needed the services of a doctor to determine why I was having groin pain. I dowsed all the possibilities I knew without determining the actual problem. My High Self determined the medical building for me to search out the needed doctor. While looking at the medical directory, my High Self selected the doctor. When the receptionist asks me who referred me to the doctor, I said, "I dowsed the doctor from the directory." She was surprised, however, but she knew what dowsing was and this led into a nice conversation. The doctor determined that I had a small hernia.

One of my objectives is to encourage healthcare practitioners to become dowsers. It is my belief they will do a better job of diagnosing and prescribing medications to their patients when they dowse. Dowsing will help them verify their patient's problem and then, using their medical training, assist them in determining the best healthcare treatment.

A few years ago while seeing an acupuncturist, the doctor wanted to use a larger needle on my third appointment. I asked him how he determined the best needle size to use for each patient. He said, "I don't know." He commented that he starts with one size and monitors the patient's progress. If the progress is not up to his expectation, he switches to a different needle size. My body could not handle the larger needle size.

I mentioned to him that if he learned how to dowse, he would know the correct needle size to use for each patient from the first treatment. That piqued his interest. Shortly after learning how to dowse, he moved to another state. This was disappointing to me because I was hoping to monitor his progress to verify his success.

FOOD

As a dowser, you should *never* get food poisoning again. You should always dowse the safety of food before it is eaten.

Have you ever wondered whether the food in your refrigerator is safe to eat? All leftover food from your refrigerator should be dowsed whether it is safe to eat. This has saved me from getting food poisoning many times.

You should always dowse the safety of food before it is eaten at a restaurant. Better yet, have your High

Self research the safety of food before you place your order. On two occasions, the food served me was not thoroughly cooked. Dowsing the food before eating prevented me from possibly getting sick.

When there is more than one item on the menu that is tempting you, ask your High Self to determine if the potential food choices are safe to eat. If you get a *Yes* response, then ask which food item would you enjoy the most. That's the one you order.

When going through a cafeteria or buffet line, dowse the safety of each food item before taking it. This is where the eye blink system (deviceless dowsing) provides a quick response to determine the safety of your food choices.

To quickly determine the safety of food, you can create another contract with your High Self. First, get permission to do so. Then establish the key words that trigger your contract. For me, I only want to mention to my High Self, **"Is this food safe for me to eat?"** When this phrase is recited, the food is compared against my established parameters.

My parameters are: Am I allergic to the food that I want to order, or I am about to eat? Will the food cause a detrimental reaction to my body? Do I have a food sensitivity to what I am about to eat? Will my body be able to easily digest the food? You may come up with some additional questions you want to include in your list of parameters.

It is also a good idea to bless and energize the food to be eaten. This is especially important if the food has been microwaved. My dowsing tells me that microwaves destroy much of the food energy. Blessing the food helps reinstall this energy to the food. You may want to recite these two blessings before eating your food. The first is a numerology blessing of "995." The first 9 represents the trinity (Father, Son & Holy Spirit) squared. The second 9 stands for completion. The 5 represents our body. These numbers help energize food. The second blessing is to say, "Dear God, I give thanks for the food I am about to eat. Please bless and energize the food for my highest nutritional value." Sometimes when saying this blessing with my hands over my food, they will jerk. It is like putting a bolt of energy into the food. When the energy of food or water is dowsed before and after these blessings, the energy value is always increased.

You may like to use the food blessings from Joey Korn instead. Here is his prayer: "If it be Thy Will, may the Powers of Nature converge to increase and enhance the beneficial energies in this room (or at this table) to maximize the nutritional value of this food we are about to eat. May these energies make this food easily digestible, highly enjoyable, and of right and perfect benefit to each individual here today (tonight). Amen."

An easy way to dowse the energy value of food is to use *Chart 1 – Numbers* and *Yes / No Chart* located in the Appendix section of this book, or you can use your fingers. The chart contains a numerical scale from one to ten with one being the lowest value and ten the highest. Ask your High Self to *Research* the energy value of the food for your highest and best good. When using Chart 1, have your High Self point your pendulum to the respective number.

Your fingers represent a chart that is always with you. In using your fingers, ask your High Self, "Is the energy value greater than five?" If a *No* response is received, count your fingers from one to five, starting from the small finger and moving toward your thumb. If you want to start from your thumb and count towards your small finger, that is also okay. Hold your pendulum over the top of your wrist and ask your High Self to point to the correct finger, which represent the energy value of the food. If a *Yes* response was received to "the energy value being greater than five," then have your little finger represent a six and your thumb a ten. Your pendulum will point to the energy value of the food for your highest and best good.

FOOD SUPPLEMENTS

My day begins by dowsing which vitamins, minerals and herbs my body needs. I establish a contract with my High Self based upon important parameters desired in my vitamins, minerals and herbs. These parameters are triggered by the phrase, **"Is this supplement safe to consume?"** My important parameters are: the vitamins, minerals and herbs must be of the highest quality; highest life force; no fillers; no adverse side effects; and my body must be able to easily and safely assimilate them. You can implement a similar contract with your High Self based on your important parameters.

With the contract in place, ask your High Self these questions, "Do I need this supplement at this time? How many capsules or tablets do I take at this time?" You can use *Chart 1 – Numbers* and *Yes/No Chart* or your fingers for this information. Your High Self will tell you so you won't over medicate and waste your supplements. You can also ask, "Do I take these vitamins, minerals and herbs with a meal or between meals?" Some supplements are recommended for taking with meals and others between meals. The next question is "Can I take all the supplements that I need daily together?" Sometimes your High Self will tell you that certain vitamins, minerals and herbs are needed, but it does not automatically mean they can all be consumed at the same time. Some supplements may not be compatible.

When shopping for supplements, ask your High Self which manufacturer's brand is the most beneficial for your body. As indicated in the previous food section, use your fingers and the scale of one to ten. One represents the worst for you while ten is the very best. This way you only purchase the supplements that your body can absorb and will have the most beneficial energy impact on your health. When you find more than one brand of vitamins, minerals and herbs that dowse high, place the two or more bottles side by side. If you do not want to use a pendulum, relax your arm. Ask your High Self to move your arm and point to the bottle that is the best for you from this group.

LABYRINTHS

About five years ago, I met a lovely woman that shared to me the benefits of walking Labyrinths. A Labyrinth is a positive energy vortex consisting from three to eleven interconnecting circles. It is estimated that man began creating Labyrinths around 2,000 BC. The earliest recorded existence of a Labyrinth comes from the Mycenaean Palace at Pylos, located in southern Greece around 1200 BC. The Labyrinth symbol was engraved on the coins produced at Knossos, Crete from the first and second century BC. The Labyrinth symbol was also important to many of the Arizona and New Mexico Indian tribes. It represents the journey through life.

The eleven-circle French Chartres Labyrinth contains incredible energy. However the seven-circle Cretan Labyrinth is the most popular. Grace Cathedral in San Francisco has a French Chartres Labyrinth that contains powerful energy. The energy emitted from the Labyrinth was very calming, soothing and peaceful. Maybe being in the Cathedral had something to do with it, but I felt connected to Spirit during and after walking it.

The seven circles of the Cretan Labyrinth correspond to the seven major chakras of the body. Walking a Labyrinth helps to balance the left and right brains, reduce stress, and some people have experienced a health healing.

My desire to purchase a new home with the backyard large enough to accommodate a Labyrinth came true a few years ago. I dowsed the exact location for the Labyrinth, its entrance point and whether it should be a left or right hand opening. It is believed that a left hand opening is female orientated energy and right signifies male. The opening to my Labyrinth is right handed.

It was important to me that my Labyrinth be powerful in its energy healing and benefit the public as well as myself. I acquired flat, jagged rocks from a Sedona, Arizona rock quarry. Most Labyrinths that I have walked, place round river rocks on top of the ground. I did not want this look for my Labyrinth. I dug trenches in all seven circles to partially bury the rocks. The jagged rock features give my Labyrinth an interesting beauty. My High Self communicated to me five thought-form procedures, which I performed on my Labyrinth to increase its energy. Everyone that has walked my Labyrinth has commented on how he or she can feel the energy and how relaxed he or she feels after walking it. My High Self indicated that forty-five minutes was the maximum time a person should spend inside it before the energy became overpowering. My Labyrinth is the only one I know where this short time period has been determined. It is very gratifying to know that my powerful Labyrinth is helping people.

FENG SHUI

An area that is currently captivating my interest is Feng Shui (pronounced fung-shway). It is an old Chinese practice of placing things throughout the home, business and landscape to enhance energy flow.

Feng means wind and *Shui* means water.

My recommendation for Feng Shui practitioners is to learn dowsing because it will improve their effectiveness. A Feng Shui consultant may make recommendations to move an object to a location, paint this area a certain color, purchase objects to help move or block energy, etc. While all these recommendations are good, a Feng Shui/dowser consultant will say something like, "Move this object to this *exact* location, paint this area this *exact* color of purple, purchase a mirror and place it exactly at this spot above your door," etc.

A very good friend of mine, who is a Feng Shui consultant and a dowser, mentioned to me one day that I should put something purple in my wealth corner, which was confirmed by her dowsing. The wealth corner is the upper left-hand corner of a room or yard. She was going to leave it up me as to what this purple object would be. Since I was a dowser, she knew I would dowse the exact location for it.

While attending a landscape conference, I heard a landscape architect mention and explain how the use of color can add interest and appeal to a yard. The slides I saw convinced me that this is what I wanted to do with my backyard. My dowsing indicated that I should paint my wealth corner purple.

My first reaction to painting my block fence corner purple was, would it be overwhelming? Would it be more of a distraction than an asset? However, I do trust my dowsing process. So, while at the paint store, I dowsed the exact color of purple for my fence corner.

Now, I'm like a proud father showing off a newborn

baby when I tell people about my purple corner. When people come over to see my landscape, they comment on how great the purple corner looks. The shadows of cactus and other plants against the purple wall add so much interest and caricature to my landscape. Energy-sensitive people can easily feel the energy emitted from this corner. I can definitely say it has had a positive impact on my financial situation.

The next color added to my fence was a pale yellow. Again, I dowsed the exact color of yellow to use. It looks great and compliments the purple. My goal now is to paint my entire block fence. I plan on adding a light green to the left side for my health and family area, light blue on the right side for my creativity side, pale pink in the upper right-hand corner for my love and marriage area, and maybe a small red section in the middle of my block fence for my fame and reputation area. People have also commented on how spiritual my backyard is becoming. The colors used on my fence are an innovative use of the Feng Shui techniques.

I also used my dowsing to determine the exact location for hanging a gemstone mobile from the ceiling of my home. Again, a Feng Shui consultant would say, "Place it in a certain area." Through my dowsing, I now have it in its exact location for enhancing the energy in my home. I recently purchased some pictures that I dowsed would help create great energy in my home. When I get ready to hang them, I know they will be in placed in the best room, on the appropriate wall, and in the exact location.

This Feng Shui experience has confirmed one of my earlier statements made in my book. *Whatever you do, dowsing will enable you to do it better.*

PLANTS

I find that dowsing your plants is a good way to help them look their best. First of all, I have my High Self, who is working with my landscape expert spirit, research the characteristics of the plant. Then I dowse where in my yard a plant should be planted for its health and esthetic design. This helps ensure the right plant for the right location. Some plants may appreciate more or less sunlight for their optimum health. When I'm planting a plant, I dowse which direction the plant would prefer to face. This I feel helps it to grow better. I also dowse each day if there is a plant that needs to be watered. If so, I find out which one(s) and I make sure to water it.

If you have some plants in your yard that are not doing very well, here are some tips to follow. Dowse to see if the plant is located in a noxious energy zone. Some plants do not grow well in these noxious energy zones. If you get a *Yes* response, ask your High Self if the noxious energy zone should either be removed or filled with beneficial energy.

Once you have determined that your plant is not in a noxious energy zone, ask the plant if it has a vital life force or whether its life force is weak. If the plant does not have a vital life force, ask your High Self to assign one to it. If its vital life force is weak, ask your High Self if its force can be increased to its optimum level. Once the problem has been corrected, you should enjoy much healthier plants.

When it comes to pruning my trees, I ask my High Self to work with an expert arborist spirit. I dowse which branches should be removed for the overall appearance and health of the tree. The same thing applies when I'm fertilizing my plants. I ask my High Self if the mixture is the correct strength for the health of my plants.

With my yard looking so great, my goal is for it to be professionally photographed and published in Sunset Magazine, plus other publications.

DIRECTIONS

As a dowser, you should *never* get lost again. All you need to do is ask your High Self, "What direction is magnetic north?" Check with your High Self to determine if it understands directions that a compass indicates. If it does, then you will always be given the direction you request.

Let's use the following as an example. You are hiking and you are lost. If you have a dowsing instrument, you can easily determine a certain direction. You can also ask your High Self to point to the direction your vehicle is parked or to the nearest civilization. If you do not have a dowsing instrument with you, find a tree branch that forms a Y-shape. Remove the leaves from this branch. You now have a dowsing instrument (Y-rod) to help you find your way. Remember, you need to determine your *Yes* and *No* responses with each dowsing instrument. The Y-rod points down for my *Yes* response and up toward me for my *No* response.

Don't forget deviceless dowsing. Relax your arm and use it to determine a certain direction like north or where your vehicle is parked.

MISSING ITEMS

From time to time, we misplace things like our car keys and spend hours looking for them. Dowsing can help simplify locating misplaced items.

Let's use misplaced car keys as an example. You want to picture in your mind what the key or the keychain looks like. With this information, you are ready to dowse. Using an L-rod, or a pendulum, ask your High Self to *Research* where the keys are located. I recommend that your first question to your High Self be, "Do you know where the keys are located?" With a *Yes* response, you are ready to locate them.

Through the process of elimination, reduce the area to a manageable size.

Start out by asking if the keys are outside your home. If your High Self gives you a *No* response, then ask if they are inside your home. Let's assume your High Self gives you a *Yes* response. Then go through the rooms of your house, eliminating those rooms with a *No* response. Let's also assume that the keys are in a dresser drawer located in the master bedroom. When your High Self gives you a *Yes* response to the keys being in your master bedroom, stand in the middle of the room and ask which direction do you walk to find the missing car keys. The L-rod will then point to your dresser. When you get to the dresser, ask if the keys are on top of the dresser. With a *No* response, ask if the keys are in one of the dresser drawers. Your L-rod will give you a *Yes* response. Next ask which drawer. When your High Self indicates the respective drawer, pull out the drawer and look for the car keys. It is important to realize that if you received *No* responses to the keys being on top of the dresser or in any of the dresser drawers, then ask if the keys are on the floor. They may have fallen behind the dresser.

LOST AND MISSING PEOPLE

Dowsers can provide a valuable service in locating lost and missing people. Their dowsing skills may result in saving lives. If the missing person is an adult, it is my recommendation that you get approval from the missing person's High Self before trying to locate them. Why? Some people may not want to be found. To locate them is an invasion of their privacy. The exception is whether the person violated the law or is dead.

Let's use the example of a child being kidnapped. The first question to ask your High Self, "Is the child alive?" You may need to expand this question by saying something like, "Is this child alive based upon their incarnated body in their current physical life on Planet Earth?" Your High Self has to know that it is this present life we are asking about and not a different life. Some dowsers use the statement "zero time" or "in my time clock now." This answer helps determine the urgency in locating the child. If the child is dead, dowse to locate the body by using the same procedure for locating people that are alive.

Assuming the child is alive, continue by asking, "Is the child in the state of their recorded address?" If the response is *No*, the child could be anywhere. Divide the country down to its smallest area. For example, "Right now, is the child east or west of the Mississippi?" Remember, all two-part questions are divided into single questions. "Is the child in the northern states or the southern states?" Then you can dowse state by state. Once the state has been determined, draw an imaginary line across the map of the state and ask, "Can the child be found in the northern or southern part of the state?" Draw another imaginary line from the top to the bottom of the state. Ask, "Can the child be found in the eastern part or western part of the state?" The state can be divided until you have determined the City/Town. Once you know the City/Town, follow the same process by reducing it down to its smallest workable area. An experienced professional dowser should be able to locate the house number. See next section on Map Dowsing for another process of locating people.

MAP DOWSING

Map dowsing becomes a quick way to locate a person or thing. Using the above example, place a ruler along either side of the state map. Instruct your High Self to move your pendulum in a *No* response, or any response you prefer, as you move the ruler across the state. When the ruler comes across the spot where the missing person or thing is located, instruct your High Self to change your pendulum to a *Yes* response. Draw a line across the state map. Next, if you started at the top or bottom of the page, now move the ruler to either side of the state map. Again, while your pendulum is moving in a *No* response, move the ruler across the state. When the ruler comes across the spot where the missing person or thing is located, your pendulum will change to a *Yes* response. Another line is drawn across the state. Where the two lines intersect is the location of the missing person or thing. Try it and see if it works for you.

BURIED TREASURE

Locating buried treasure can be a fun and exciting process using your dowsing skills. However, before you enthusiastically go looking for buried treasure, there is some important information you need to know. Otherwise, you may be digging some empty holes.

My recommendation is to read some books on treasure dowsing, like the *Dowser's Treasure Hunting Manual* by Louis Matacia. Some dowsers may find it helpful to use a witness L-rod or pendulum. These dowsing instruments contain a sample of what they are looking for within the instrument. A small gold nugget or dust may be beneficial in locating gold coins.

It is also my recommendation that you have permission to dowse for the buried treasure. Buried treasure is doing no one any good being buried, and many people feel that finders are keepers. However, maybe some buried treasure is better served being in a museum for all to enjoy, rather than in your possession, i.e., Indian pottery and artifacts. Once you get permission to locate the treasure, go for it.

Next, check to determine if there are any blocks or interferences in locating buried treasure on the established site. For example, if the person who buried the treasure understood the power of thought-form energy, you will never find it, unless you also understand thought-forms. When a person buries a treasure, the energy of the buried item can be transferred to another location. If a dowser taps into that thought-form energy, many dry holes will be dug. Ask your High Self if there is a thought-form protecting the buried treasure. This thought-form is the transference of the buried treasurer's energy to another location. If a *Yes* response is received, ask if the thought-form can be removed. With a *Yes* response, ask your High Self to remove the thought form. (See Chapter Seven on Clearing Blocks and Interferences.) Now, ask if the true buried treasure can be located. With a *Yes* response, you are ready to dowse for it. Map dowsing is one way to locate buried treasure. Where the lines intersect, then becomes a similar procedure as has been described with water dowsing.

In demonstrating this procedure in community college classes, I place my wallet with money in it on the floor. I ask my High Self to locate the money that is in my wallet. Using my L-rods, they cross in front of me when they are over my wallet. I place another object, i.e., a book or my pendulum pouch, a few feet away from my wallet. With my hands placed over my wallet, I ask my High Self to transfer the energy of my money located in my wallet to the object. Extending my hands outward like they are holding the energy of my money, I make a quick movement of my hands over the other object on the floor. When I ask my High Self to locate my money, I can stand over my wallet and my L-rods will not move. However, they will cross in front of me when I'm standing over the other object on the floor. When I have my High Self clear the thought-form, my L-rods will cross again when I'm standing over my wallet.

JEWELRY

A few years ago, while seeing my chiropractor for an adjustment, she asked me if I was wearing a crystal on a chain around my neck. I was very amazed that she knew this, since I had never told her, and I always remove the crystal before receiving an adjustment. I replied that I do wear a crystal. She asked me to get my crystal and place it around my neck. Through muscle testing, she asked whether the crystal was being worn over the proper chakra. My response to her muscle testing was a definite *No*. The chain on my crystal had it hanging over my heart chakra and muscle testing indicated that over my throat chakra would be a better place for me. Dowsing would have given me the same information had I known it was important to check this out.

This experience taught me a very valuable lesson.

Many people wear crystals or certain jewelry because it is fashionable or to supposedly increase their energy. Before wearing any jewelry, dowse the beneficial effects to you. This also applies to wearing a watchband. You might find it interesting to determine the best metal to have against your skin. Is it silver, gold or is a leather band the best?

Wearing magnets can promote the healing of a person's body if used correctly. However, before purchasing them, dowse to determine whether wearing a magnet is good for you. For me, wearing a magnetic bracelet dowsed out a positive nine on a scale from one to ten. If you dowse this for yourself, don't stop after this question. Ask each day, what wrist should you wear the bracelet over, what direction should the magnets face, and how many hours a day can you safely wear it? You can also ask for how long a time period (weeks, months, or years) you should wear the magnetic bracelet. Wearing the magnetic bracelet did help reduce the pain in my fingers.

Most magnet salespeople comment that magnets are beneficial to a person's health. While this statement is generally true, my dowsing indicates that magnets can be detrimental if used incorrectly. Before using a magnet, determine which direction each polarity should be facing. Measure the energy impact of each magnet on your body before selecting it by using *Chart 1 – Numbers* and *Yes / No Chart*. Sometimes the strongest magnet is not always the best one for you. Being a dowser, you know how to maximize the effectiveness of using magnets.

BURIED PIPES AND ELECTRICAL LINES

Being a dowser saves time and effort in locating buried irrigation pipes, sewer pipes, electrical lines, etc. For example, in dowsing for a buried irrigation line, picture in your mind the type of pipe—PVC or polyethylene—you want found. Sometimes, holding a piece of the type of pipe you are requesting to locate can be helpful. I first have my High Self *Research* below the ground for the requested pipe or electrical line. Next, I ask my High Self if it understands my request. Then I ask, "Is the pipe there?" With a *Yes* response, we are ready to proceed.

Pipes can be side by side. By focusing on the type of pipe desired, your High Self will pass over the pipe not needed, to locate the pipe you requested. When the line is located, your L-rods will either cross or open outward. Each pipe has a different vibration and your request taps into the correct vibration. It is amazing how this works.

Once you have located the desired pipe, ask your High Self to trace the pipe's path. Walk in the direction the L-rods indicate. In following the L-rods, they can determine the turns in the pipe and the side branching lines by the direction they move. You can even request how deep the pipes are buried. This is determined by selecting a beginning number that reflects the depth in inches. Then with a pendulum or L-rod, increase or decrease the number until you dowsing instrument gives you the correct depth. To determine where there is a break or leak in your pipe, ask your High Self to have your L-rods cross in front of you, or open outward, when the break or leak has been located.

Another practical example is dowsing to locate a buried PVC sleeve under the driveway. Most new homebuilders install a PVC sleeve under the driveway for the benefit of homeowners. These sleeves allow irrigation pipes or electrical lines to be slid under the driveway for servicing the opposite side. My experience with homebuilders is they state an approximate distance from the garage along with its buried depth for the location of this sleeve. Many hours can be spent digging in trying to locate this sleeve. As a dowser, you can easily determine its location and depth.

VOTING

Even though my intentions are to become an informed voter, I do not have the time to keep up-to-date on all the issues or the candidates. Therefore, when it comes to voting, I ask my High Self to select the best candidate and whether I should vote for or against an issue.

For candidates, I have my High Self *Research* them from my established parameters. These parameters are honesty, ethics, knowledge, and a willingness to serve the public. When I receive my sample ballot, I hold it sideways and have my High Self point my pendulum to the name of the candidate that I should vote for based upon these established parameters. Isn't this a much better way of voting for a candidate than basing it upon appearance or party affiliation?

Some propositions can be very confusing to understand. Therefore, I have my High Self *Research* the pros and cons of each as they apply to what is best for the people. With this information, I ask my High Self whether I should vote for or against the proposition.

BOOKS/SPEAKERS

Have you read a book or heard a speaker that had an impact on you? The information was taken in and made a part of your belief system because it sounded so convincing. Just because the information was convincing, should not mean that you automatically believe it without checking its accuracy. The information may be the *truth* of the author or speaker because that is their belief system, but it may not be your *truth*.

As a dowser, you should always check out someone's information before you make it your *truth*. The information presented in this book is my *truth*. Use *Chart 1 – Numbers* and *Yes / No Chart* to dowse the accuracy of the information for yourself. If more people did this, we would not have people following a leader that results in people doing something they may regret later.

When reading or hearing some convincing information, dowse it for accuracy for the author or speaker, against universal (Spiritual) consciousness and your consciousness. First, dowse the accuracy of the information as it applies to the author or speaker. The information may be 100 percent accurate for the author but only 60 percent accurate according to spiritual consciousness or your consciousness. If the accuracy of the information dowses higher for spiritual consciousness than your consciousness, check as to whether you have an incorrect belief system regarding the information. If you do, then the choice is yours if you want to change your belief. You want your consciousness to equal that of Spirit.

CARS/TRUCKS

Dowsing can save you money when it comes to the maintenance of your car or truck. You can determine how many more miles can be accumulated on your brakes before replacing them. Before taking your vehicle on a trip, dowse to determine whether there is anything that needs to be repaired. You do not want to be stranded along some highway. When you take your vehicle in for repairs, dowse the accuracy of the information the mechanic is giving you regarding what needs to be repaired. You do not want to pay for unnecessary repairs.

Recently, I took my truck in for an oil change at a quick oil change franchise. An employee showed me on a plastic card what my transmission fluid looked like and an example of what it should look like. He said for an additional charge, they would change the fluid. I quickly dowsed using my eyes as to whether I was being told the truth. I received a *No* response. So

I just had them change my oil. I don't plan on using them again.

PICTURES/ANTIQUES

Before any picture/poster is hung in your home, you should dowse to determine whether it is energy enhancing or draining. You can use *Chart 1 – Numbers* and *Yes/No Chart* for assistance. If a picture is energy draining, ask your High Self if it can be neutralized. You can use your *Clearing* response for this procedure.

I'm concerned about some of the symbolic death/ evil posters that children hang in their bedroom. My dowsing indicates these posters can have a detrimental impact on their personality. This impact can be the loss of respect for another life. If parents do not get them removed, they can dowse for approval to have their High Self neutralize the detrimental energy coming from these posters.

Antiques are still popular with many people. However, they should be dowsed and cleared of detrimental energy, just the same as pictures, before bringing them into your home. If an antique comes from an angry/hateful environment, this detrimental energy can become attached to it. Bringing this detrimental energy into your home is not the best choice.

ELECTRICAL DEVICES

Although electrical devices make life more comfortable and productive, they can produce a negative electrical energy field that can be detrimental to one's health. As a dowser, you will be able to locate these negative energy fields and either neutralize them by placing a thought-form shield around them or simply stay out of their detrimental energy area.

Computers are great. They make us more productive and help us communicate with the world. However, most computer terminals emit a detrimental electrical energy field, which generally extends outward to our wrist. Spending a great amount of time at a computer may result in your energy level dropping. Once you know a detrimental electrical energy field exists, you are able to do something about it. There are specialized products which when placed near or attached to the computer will neutralize this detrimental energy. Try placing a thought-form energy shield over the computer to protect you from this detrimental energy.

Microwave ovens should be dowsed to determine their detrimental energy field. You then can remain out of this field when it is operating or place a thought-form shield next to it as described above. Digital alarm clocks should also be checked. You do not want your head in this detrimental energy field. Either place the clock a greater distance from your head, place a neutralizing product on it, or place a thought-form shield around it.

Chapter Ten

GIVING THANKS

One way to keep your dowsing skills sharp is to give thanks to God/Spirit and your High Self when the dowsing session is over. Giving thanks is showing appreciation for the wonderful dowsing gift that was given to you. It is also a way of recognizing that you have help in your dowsing success.

To clarify this point, consider the following analogy. If you were sending gifts to me on my birthday, how long would you continue to do this if I never said thanks, never even acknowledged that I had received your gifts? Probably not very long. You would be very disappointed.

I don't want to gamble with God/Spirit, and my High Self with the possibility of losing my dowsing gift. That is why giving thanks after a dowsing session is so important to me.

Chapter Eleven

Conclusion

Now that you have a better understanding and knowledge of what dowsing is all about and how you can use it to help your life, hopefully you are excited about becoming a dowser. If you are new to dowsing, my congratulations go out to you for being assertive and inquisitive enough to read this book.

Dowsing opens us to the knowledge of the universe and all we have to do is tap into it. It really is that easy. Remember that you can dowse for anything as long as you have permission and will not cause harm to any person, animal or the environment. This knowledge is there to assist us in making better decisions about our life and to help us take control over it.

It is important to understand that we are the dowsing instrument and our power, our knowledge comes from the God-source. Dowsing instruments help us visually to understand and gain more confidence in the answers to our questions.

Dowsing is a wonderful tool to help you in all areas of your life. It should not be feared or ridiculed.

The wonderful thing about dowsing is that it is positive, valuable, and informative and it will be a great addition to your life. You do not have to give up anything to get this.

I mentioned that dowsers are in the brain wave states of Beta, Alpha, Theta and Delta simultaneously. What a great way to develop our minds and our psychic abilities. Your body also talks to you through what we call our intuition, which is that gut feeling, or that voice in your head. When you sense this intuition or hear that voice, please honor it because it is your body dowsing your truth. Sometimes this intuitive voice is very faint and can easily be over ridden by our conscious awareness. When you listen to and follow your intuition or that voice, don't you feel great? Dowsing enables you to easily and confidently communicate with your High Self all the time.

Everything on this planet has a vibration and every vibration is different. When we want to know something, we dowse or ask for the "knowingness" to our question. This gets us in touch with the God-source energy. The energy from this vibration comes into our super sensitive crown chakra, one of the seven main chakras or energy points in our body. Our High Self works in harmony with our subconscious mind, which makes our dowsing instrument move. This is how the "knowingness" of the *truth* impacts our five senses of touch, taste, sight, smell and hearing.

Dowsing also enables us to take back our power rather than give it away to others to make decisions regarding our life. For example, when it comes to your health, you now have a tool to help you make better decisions about it. You, your High Self and your doctor work as a team for your improved health. As more healthcare practioners become dowsers, they will draw upon their education and training to verify their health diagnoses with their High Self for recommending the best health treatment for their patients.

You are embarking on a wonderful journey that will help you become more spiritual, healthy and happy with your life. This journey will amaze you with the wealth of information revealed to you.

If you get involved in service to others using your dowsing skills, you will feel great joy and satisfaction. Realizing the spiritual/energy connection between people is very humbling as you see and feel the power of God working with you and through you to help others. The exciting thing about dowsing is that it comes from the God-source and it has always been available to us. Everyone who wants to learn it can do so. However, not everyone chooses to develop the necessary skill to be really effective.

Dowsing will not cost you a lot of money to learn. The main cost is for purchasing dowsing instruments and possibly taking some dowsing classes. There is no ritual or ceremony of acceptance. While we call it dowsing, we could have called it energy connection, spiritual awareness, knowledge of the universe, and so on. What is important is that we have a tool that expands our awareness of the universe and improves our lives.

Once you start dowsing, you will come to the awareness that many of us have realized in that you wished *you would have learned dowsing years ago.* Enjoy your journey.

Appendix

Chart dowsing is a quick and easy way to get information. There are many dowsing books with great charts in them to help you determine information for making better decisions about your life. There are fixed charts, which contain information that you refer to on a frequent basis, i.e., vitamin and herb charts. Some dowsers like to take a blank chart and create their own words in it thereby making it flexible to their needs. When it comes to using charts, I recommend that you talk to your High Self as to how you want to use them. Listed below are my recommendations for using the attached charts.

Chart 1 – Number and Yes/No Chart

This chart has multiple uses. You can use this chart to obtain your *Yes* and *No* responses. Place your pendulum on the black dot and ask your High Self to move it up and down for your *Yes* response and side to side for your *No*.

When using this chart for general information, mention to your High Self that a plus 10, or 100, means the best for you. Any number less than 10, or 100, means a decreasing effectiveness for you.

Here is an example of how I use this chart. When purchasing vitamins or herbs, I dowse to determine the energy effectiveness in my body. I only want to purchase vitamins or herbs that come close to a plus 10/100. Then I determine how many capsules or tablets I need from a certain vitamin or herb. Do not be surprised if your pendulum goes to the minus numbers when dowsing prescription drugs.

Number and Yes/No Chart

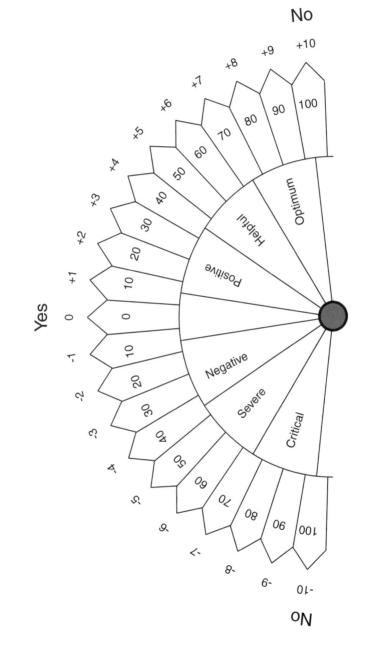

Chart 2 – Alphabet Chart

I like to use this chart to help me spell words. First, I ask my High Self if it knows the word. Then I ask what is the first letter, then the next, and next until my pendulum flat-lines, which is a *No* response. I then double-check the word by asking my High Self if this word is spelled correctly.

Alphabet Chart

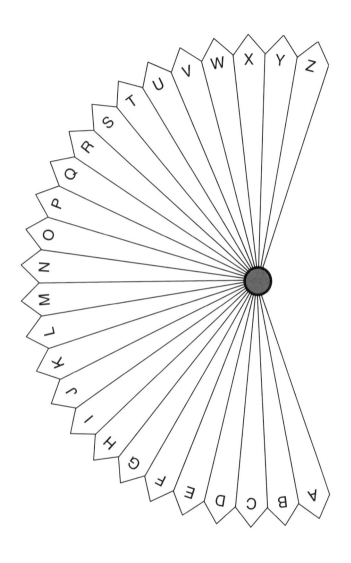

Chart 3 – Color Chart

When using the Color Chart, ask if you need the energy vibration of a certain color added to you at this time. If you get a *Yes* response, have your High Self apply it to you. Your pendulum should start spinning. When it stops, ask if the energy vibration has been applied.

I like to use this chart to determine what is the proper color to wear today to keep my energy in balance. First have your High Self *Research* your present wardrobe. I use my slacks as my dominant color indicated by the Color Chart. You could have your High Self determine the colors you need and then you can add them to your wardrobe. Try this and see for yourself if your energy level is greater.

Color Chart

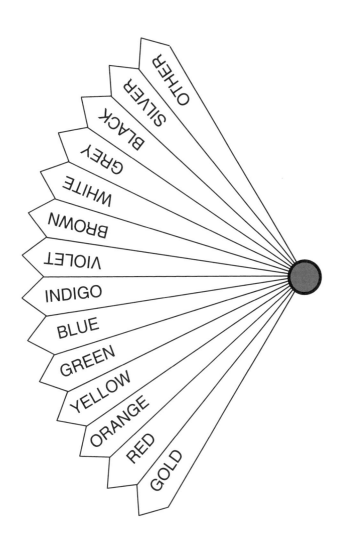

Charts 4 and 5 Blank Charts

These two charts are blank charts, which give you the opportunity to customize these charts in ways that become useful to you. For example, you could call one chart an herb chart. Just write in the names of common herbs you take regularly. Once your chart is completed, place your pendulum on the black dot. By asking your High Self which herbs you presently need, it will move your pendulum and point to the herbs.

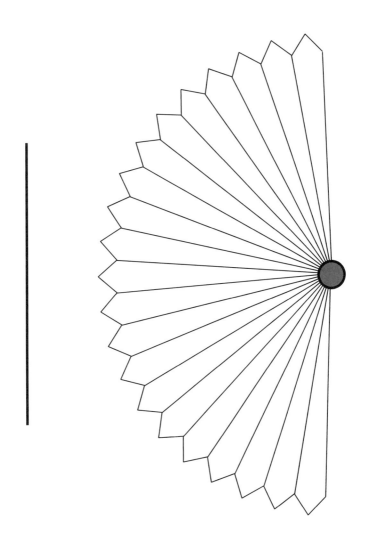

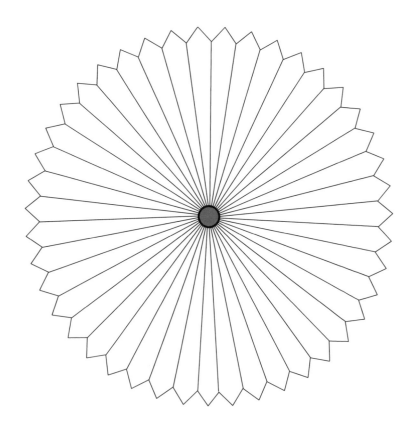

For more information about dowsing, contact:

The American Society of Dowsers
P.O. Box 24
Danville, Vermont 05828
802-684-3417
E-mail Address: ASD@dowsers.org
Website: http://www.asd.dowsers.org

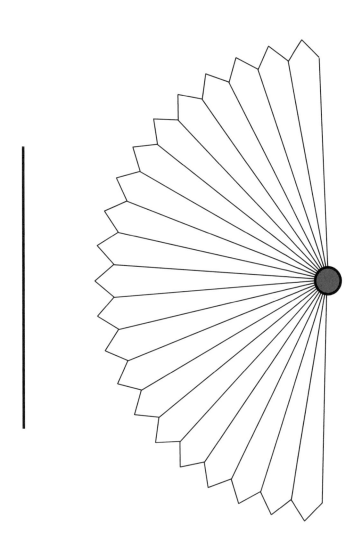

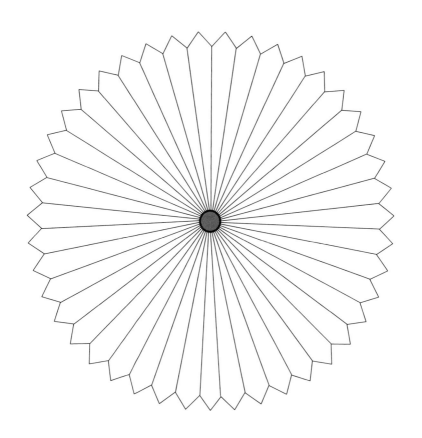

BIBLIOGRAPHY

Ater, Bob, *King Tutankhamens Pendulum*, The American Dowser Quarterly Digest, Spring 1999.

December 1998 New Zealand Society of Dowsing & Radionics, *How Dowsing Got Its Name*, The American Dowser Quarterly Digest, Spring 1999.

Detzler, Robert E., *Soul Re-Creation, Developing Your Cosmic Potential*, SRC Publishing, 1994.

The Holy Bible, New Revised Standard Version, 1989.

Korn, Joseph, *Dowsing: A Path to Enlightenment*, New Millennium Press, 1999.

Saward, Jeff, *Ancient Labyrinths of The World*, Caerdroia Publishing, 1998.

Stillman, Ed, *Dowser's Brainwave Characteristics Part Two: Brainwave Coherence and Delta Waves*, The American Dowser Quarterly Digest, Spring 1998.

Stillman, Ed, - *New Research on Dowser's Brainwave Characteristics*, The American Dowser Quarterly Digest, Winter 1997.

Weil, Andrew, M.D., *Sound Body, Sound Mind: Music for Healing*, 1997.

Woods, Walt, *Letter to Robin, a Mini-Course in Pendulum Dowsing*, Walter Woods, June 1995.

NOTES

NOTES

NOTES

NOTES